Berl

Mar
Chinese

phrase book & dictionary

Berlitz Publishing
New York   London   Singapore

Contacting the Editors
Every effort has been made to provide accurate information in this publication, but changes are inevitable. The publisher cannot be responsible for any resulting loss, inconvenience or injury. We would appreciate it if readers would call our attention to any errors or outdated information. We also welcome your suggestions; if you come across a relevant expression not in our phrase book, please contact us at: **comments@berlitzpublishing.com**

All Rights Reserved
© 2018 Apa Digital (CH) AG and Apa Publications (UK) Ltd.
Berlitz Trademark Reg. U.S. Patent Office and other countries. Marca Registrada. Used under license from Berlitz Investment Corporation.

Ninth Printing: August 2018
Printed in China

Editor: Helen Fanthorpe
Translation: updated by Wordbank
Cover Design: Rebeka Davies
Interior Design: Beverley Speight
Picture Researcher: Tom Smyth

Cover Photos: iStock and Shutterstock
Interior Photos: Crowne Piazza Shanghai 47; APA Alex Havret 103, 111; APA David Henley 1, 81, 136, 143; Hyatt on the Bund 41; Fotolia 59; APA Lucy Johnston 168; APA Shen Kai 141; APA Ryan Pyle 14, 21, 24, 38, 60, 70, 73, 96, 99, 117, 121, 127; APA Ming Tang Evans 64, 77, 105, 106

Distribution

UK, Ireland and Europe
Apa Publications (UK) Ltd
sales@insightguides.com
United States and Canada
Ingram Publisher Services
ips@ingramcontent.com
Australia and New Zealand
Woodslane
info@woodslane.com.au
Southeast Asia
Apa Publications (SN) Pte
singaporeoffice@insightguides.com

Worldwide
Apa Publications (UK) Ltd
sales@insightguides.com

Special Sales, Content Licensing, and CoPublishing
Discounts available for bulk quantities. We can create special editions, personalized jackets, and corporate imprints. sales@insightguides.com; www.insightguides.biz

Contents

Food & Drink

People

Leisure Time

Special Requirements

In an Emergency

Dictionary

Pronunciation

The romanized pronunciation system widely used for Chinese is called **pīnyīn**, **pīnyīn**. Not all **pīnyīn** letters or letter combinations are pronounced as they normally are in English. A guide to the pronunciation of **pīnyīn** follows.

In addition to the Roman alphabet, **pīnyīn** also features tonal marks, which represent four Mandarin Chinese tones:

Tone	Simplified Mark	Description	Example	Chinese	Translation
1st	ˉ	high and level	**mā**	妈	mother
2nd	´	starts medium in tone, then rises to the top	**má**	麻	hemp
3rd	ˇ	starts low at level 2, dips to the bottom and then rises toward the top to level 4	**mǎ**	马	horse
4th	`	starts at the top and then falls sharp and strong to the bottom	**mà**	骂	scold

Vowels without tonal marks are considered 'neutral' or fifth tone:

neutral	flat, with no emphasis	**ma**	吗
		an expression of mood	

Initial Consonants

The following table illustrates the initial sounds in **pīnyīn** and their equivalents in English.

Symbol	Approximate Pronunciation	Example	Pronunciation
c	like ts in pits	草	*cǎo*
ch	like ch in church	吃	*chī*
h	like ch in Scottish loch	花	*huā*
q	like ch in chip	旗	*qí*
r	like r in raw	人	*rén*
sh	like sh in wash, with the tongue curved at the back of the mouth	是	*shì*
x	like sh in she, with the tongue resting at the back of the lower teeth	心	*xīn*
z	like ds in kids	子	*zǐ*
zh	like j in judge	中	*zhōng*

The letters b, d, f, g, j, k, l, m, n, p, s, t, w are pronounced generally as in English.

Finals

The following table illustrates the final sounds in **pīnyīn**, and their equivalents in English.

Symbol	Approximate Pronunciation	Example	Pronunciation
a	like a in father	八	*bā*
e	like e in her	鹅	*é*
i	1. like e in me	1. 一	1. *yī*
	2. not pronounced after c, s, z	2. 此	2. *cǐ*
	3. after ch, sh, zh and r, pronounce all letters of the syllable with the tongue curled back, like i in bird	3. 吃	3. *chī*
o	like aw in awe	我	*wǒ*
u	like oo in spoon	五	*wǔ*
ü	like pronouncing you with lips pursed	女	*nǚ*
ai	like ai in aisle	爱	*ài*
an	like an in ran	安	*ān*
ang	like ang in rang	昂	*áng*
ao	like ow in how	奥	*ào*
ei	like ei in eight	类	*lèi*
en	like en in open	恩	*ēn*
eng	like en in open + g	衡	*héng*
	er like err, but with the tongue curled back and the sound coming from the back of the throat	二	*èr*
ia	like ya in yard	下	*xià*
ian	similar to yen	联	*lián*

Symbol	Approximate Pronunciation	Example	Pronunciation
iang	like ee-ang	两	*liǎng*
iao	like ee ee-ow	料	*liào*
ie	like ye in yes	列	*liè*
in	like in in thin	林	*lín*
ing	like ing in thing	龄	*líng*
iong	like ee-ong	雄	*xióng*
iu	like yo in yoga	六	*liù*
ou	like ou in dough	楼	*lóu*
ong	like oong with oo as in soon	龙	*lóng*
ua	like wah	华	*huá*
uai	similar to why	怀	*huái*
uan	like wahn	环	*huán*
uang	like wahng	黄	*huáng*
ue	like u + eh	学	*xué*
ui	similar to way	会	*huì*
un	like uan in truant	魂	*hún*
uo	similar to war	或	*huò*

There are more than one billion speakers of Mandarin Chinese.
It is the official language of the People's Republic of China (PRC),
the media in China and schools in China and Taiwan. It is one of four
official languages in Singapore.
There are many dialects of Chinese spoken throughout China and
the world, but Mandarin is the most commonly used in China as well
as Taiwan. Mandarin is known as **pǔ tōng huà** in mainland China,
literally, common speech. Besides Mandarin, there are six additional
major dialects in China, including Cantonese, which is spoken in
Guangdong, Guangxi and Hong Kong. There are also a number of ethnic
languages, such as Zhuang, Mongolian and Miao.

Written Chinese is not a combination of letters but ideograms.
Chinese is written with characters known as **hàn zì**. Each
character represents a syllable of spoken Chinese; more than 80% of
Chinese characters are actually compounds of two or more characters.
Chinese in written form can be traditional or simplified. Traditional
Chinese is used in Taiwan, Hong Kong and Singapore, though the latter
two are transitioning to simplified Chinese. Traditional Chinese has
more strokes and is written vertically in columns from right to left.
Simplified Chinese has fewer strokes and is written horizontally from
left to right. This phrase book features simplified Chinese.

How to use this Book

Sometimes you see two alternatives separated by a slash. Choose the one that's right for your situation.

ESSENTIAL

I'm on vacation [holiday]/business. 我在度假/出差。 *wǒ zài dù jià/chū chāi*

I'm going to… 我要去… *wǒ yào qù…*

I'm staying at the… Hotel. 我住在…旅馆。 *wǒ zhù zài…lǚ guǎn*

Words you may see are shown in YOU MAY SEE boxes.

YOU MAY SEE...

海关 *hǎi guān*	customs
免税物品 *miǎn shuì wù pǐn*	duty-free goods
申报物品 *shēn bào wù pǐn*	goods to declare
不需要申报 *bù xū yào shēn bào*	nothing to declare

Any of the words or phrases listed can be plugged into the sentence below.

Somewhere to Stay

Can you recommend…? 你能推荐…吗？ *nǐ néng tuī jiàn…ma*

a hotel 一家旅馆 *yì jiā lǚ guǎn*

a hostel 一间旅舍 *yì jiān lǚ shè*

a campsite 一个露营地 *yí gè lù yíng dì*

Chinese phrases appear in purple.

Pinyin pronunciation follows every Chinese entry. For more on pronunciation, see page 7.

Phone

A phone card/ prepaid phone, please	请给我一张电话卡/预付电话卡。 *qǐng gěi wǒ yì zhāng diàn huà kǎ/yù fù diàn huà kǎ*
Can I have your number?	您可以告诉我您的号码吗？*nín kě yǐ gào sù wǒ nín de hào mǎ ma*
Here's my number.	这是我的号码。*zhè shì wǒ de hào mǎ*

For Numbers, see page 160.

Related phrases can be found by going to the page number indicated.

Internet-access centers and cafes can be found in major cities in China. Many hotels offer computer and internet facilities in their business centers as well as wireless internet access in private rooms, usually for a fee.

Information boxes contain relevant country, culture and language tips.

Expressions you may hear are shown in You May Hear boxes.

YOU MAY HEAR...

您是哪位？*nín shì nǎ wèi*	Who's calling?
请稍等。*qǐng shāo děng*	Hold on.
我给您接通。*wǒ gěi nín jiē tōng*	I'll put you through.
他 *m*/她 *f* 在开会。*tā/tā zài kāi huì*	He/She is in a meeting.

When different gender forms apply, the masculine form is followed by *m*; feminine by *f*.

Color-coded side bars identify each section of the book.

Survival

Arrival & Departure

ESSENTIAL

I'm on vacation [holiday]/business.	我在度假/出差。	*wǒ zài dù jià/chū chāi*
I'm going to…	我要去…	*wǒ yào qù…*
I'm staying at the… Hotel.	我住在…旅馆。	*wǒ zhù zài…lǚ guǎn*

YOU MAY HEAR...

请出示护照。 *qǐng chū shì hù zhào*	Your passport, please.
您访问的目的是什么？ *nín fǎng wèn de mù dì shì shén me*	What's the purpose of your visit?
您住在哪里？ *nín zhù zài nǎ li*	Where are you staying?
您要呆多久？ *nín yào dāi duō jiǔ*	How long are you staying?
谁和您一起来的？ *shéi hé nín yì qǐ lái de*	Who are you here with?

Border Control

I'm just passing through.	我只是过境。	*wǒ zhǐ shì guò jìng*
I'd like to declare…	我想申报…	*wǒ xiǎng shēn bào…*
I have nothing to declare.	我不需要申报。	*wǒ bù xū yào shēn bào*

U.S. and U.K. citizens must possess a valid passport and visa, issued by the Chinese authorities, to enter China. Tour groups may be issued group visas; the paperwork in this case would be handled by the travel agency.

Before you arrive in China, you will have filled out a declaration form listing any valuables in your possession. When you leave China, you may be asked to show that you are taking with you the items listed, except for any items declared as gifts.

Contact your consulate for information on obtaining visas and for health requirements and travel advisories.

YOU MAY HEAR...

需要申报吗？ xū yào shēn bào ma	Anything to declare?
该物品必须付税。 gāi wù pǐn bì xū fù shuì	You must pay duty on this.
请打开这个包。 qǐng dǎ kāi zhè ge bāo	Open this bag.

YOU MAY SEE...

海关 hǎi guān	customs
免税物品 miǎn shuì wù pǐn	duty-free goods
申报物品 shēn bào wù pǐn	goods to declare
不需要申报 bù xū yào shēn bào	nothing to declare
护照检查 hù zhào jiǎn chá	passport control
警察 jǐng chá	police

Money

ESSENTIAL

Where's the…?	⋯在哪里？	…zài nǎ li
ATM	自动取款机	zì dòng qǔ kuǎn jī
bank	银行	yín háng
currency exchange office	货币兑换处	huò bì duì huàn chù
When does the bank open/close?	银行什么时候开门/关门？	yín háng shén me shí hou kāi mén/guān mén
I'd like to change dollars/pounds into Ren Min Bi.	我想把美元/英镑换成人民币。	wǒ xiǎng bǎ měi yuán/yīng bàng huàn chéng rén mín bì
I'd like to cash traveler's checks [cheques]	我想把旅行支票换成现金。	wǒ xiǎng bǎ lǚ xíng zhī piào huàn chéng xiàn jīn

Most major credit cards are accepted in China; however, they are accepted only in major shopping malls, stores and banks. A location that accepts credit card payment will display a credit card symbol in a visible place. Traveler's checks are accepted at most large banks in China, but you may have to pay a fee to cash them. Keep the receipt from the bank where your traveler's checks were issued; you may be asked to show the receipt when you have the checks cashed. You can change money at most banks. Some large stores provide this service as well. You can go to the Money Exchange, 外币兑换 (**wài bì duì huàn**), desk or booth, usually located near the entrance. Cash is still the preferred payment method in China. Remember to bring your passport when you want to change money.

At the Bank

I'd like to change money/get a cash advance.	我想换钱/预支现金。 *wǒ xiǎng huàn qián/yù zhī xiàn jīn*
What's the exchange rate/fee?	外币兑换率/费用是多少？ *wài bì duì huàn lǜ /fèi yòng shì duō shǎo*
I think there's a mistake.	我觉得出错了。 *wǒ jué de chū cuò le*
I lost my traveler's checks [cheques].	我丢了旅行支票。 *wǒ diū le lǚ xíng zhī piào*
My credit card...	我的信用卡… *wǒ de xìn yòng kǎ…*
was lost	丢了 *diū le*
was stolen	被偷了 *bèi tōu le*
doesn't work	不能用 *bù néng yòng*

The ATM ate my card.	自动取款机吞了我的信用卡。	
	zì dòng qǔ kuǎn jī tūn le wǒ de xìn yòng kǎ	

For Numbers, see page 160.

YOU MAY SEE...

从这里插入信用卡 *cóng zhè lǐ chā rù xìn yòng kǎ*		insert card here
取消 *qǔ xiāo*		cancel
清除 *qīng chú*		clear
进入 *jìn rù*		enter
密码 *mì mǎ*		PIN
取款 *qǔ kuǎn*		withdrawal
从支票账户取钱 *cóng zhī piào zhàng hù qǔ qián*		from checking [current] account
从储蓄账户取钱 *cóng chǔ xù zhàng hù qǔ qián*		from savings account
收据 *shōu jù*		receipt

Chinese currency 人民币 **rén mín bì (RMB)**, literally, 'people's money', is not tradable outside China. The monetary unit is the 元 **yuán**, which is divided into 角 **jiǎo** and 分 **fēn**. Bill denominations include 1, 2, 5, 10, 20, 50, 100 **yuán** and 1, 2 and 5 **jiǎo**; coins include 1, 2, 5, 10, 50, 100 **fēn**. One **yuán** is equal to 100 **fēn** while 1 **jiǎo** equals 10 **fēn**.

Getting Around

ESSENTIAL

How do I get to town?	我怎么去城里？	*wǒ zěn me qù chéng lǐ*
Where's the…?	…在哪里？	*…zài nǎ li*
airport	机场	*jī chǎng*
train [railway] station	火车站	*huǒ chē zhàn*
bus station	汽车站	*qì chē zhàn*
subway [underground] station	地铁站	*dì tiě zhàn*
How far is it?	它有多远？	*tā yǒu duō yuǎn*
Where do I buy a ticket?	我在哪里买票？	*wǒ zài nǎ li mǎi piào*
A one-way/round-trip [return] ticket to…	一张到…的单程/双程票	*yī zhāng dào…de dān chéng/shuāng chéng piào*
How much?	多少钱？	*duō shǎo qián*
Which…?	哪…？	*nǎ…*
gate	个门	*ge mén*
line	条线	*tiáo xiàn*
platform	个站台	*ge zhàn tái*
Where can I get a taxi?	我可以在哪里找到出租车？	*wǒ kě yǐ zài nǎ li zhǎo dào chū zū chē*
Take me to this address.	把我送到这个地址。	*bǎ wǒ sòng dào zhè ge dì zhǐ*
Can I have a map?	我能买一张地图吗？	*wǒ néng mǎi yì zhāng dì tú ma*

Tickets

When's the...to Beijing?	去北京的…是什么时间？	*qù běi jīng de...shì shén me shí jiān*
(first) bus	（第一班）公共汽车	*(dì yī bān) gōng gòng qì chē*
(next) flight	（下一班）飞机	*(xià yì bān) fēi jī*
(last) train	（最后一班）火车	*(zuì hòu yì bān) huǒ chē*
Where do I buy a ticket?	我在哪里买票？	*wǒ zài nǎ li mǎi piào*
One/two ticket(s), please.	请给我一张/两张票。	*qǐng gěi wǒ yì zhāng/liǎng zhāng piào*
For today/tomorrow.	要今天/明天的。	*yào jīn tiān/míng tiān de*
A...ticket.	一张…票。	*yì zhāng...piào*
one way	单程	*dān chéng*
round trip [return]	双程	*shuāng chéng*
first class	头等舱	*tóu děng cāng*
business class	商务舱	*shāng wù cāng*
economy class	经济舱	*jīng jì cāng*
The express bus/ express train, please.	请给我特快巴士/火车车票。	*qǐng gěi wǒ tè kuài bā shì/huǒ chē chē piào*

The local bus/train, please.	请给我普通巴士/火车车票 *qǐng gěi wǒ Pǔ tōng bā shì/huǒ chē chē piào*
How much?	多少钱？ *duō shǎo qián*
Is there a…discount?	…打折吗？ *…dǎ zhé ma*
child	孩子 *hái zi*
student	学生 *xué shēng*
senior citizen	老人 *lǎo rén*
tourist	游客 *yóu kè*
I have an e-ticket	我有一张电子票。 *wǒ yǒu yì zhāng diàn zǐ piào*
Can I buy a ticket on the bus/train?	我可以在公共汽车/火车上买票吗？ *wǒ kě yǐ zài gōng gòng qì chē/huǒ chē shàng mǎi piào ma*
Do I have to stamp the ticket before boarding?	我必须在上车前检票吗？ *wǒ bì xū zài shàng chē qián jiǎn piào ma*
How long is this ticket valid?	这张票多长时间有效？ *zhè zhāng piào duō cháng shí jiān yǒu xiào*
Can I return on the same ticket?	我可以用同一张票回来吗？ *wǒ kě yǐ yòng tóng yì zhāng piào huí lái ma*
I'd like to…my reservation.	我想…预定。 *wǒ xiǎng…yù dìng*
cancel	取消 *qǔ xiāo*
change	改变 *gǎi biàn*
confirm	确认 *què rèn*

For Days, see page 164.

For Time, see page 163.

Plane

Airport Transfer

How much is a taxi to the airport?	去机场坐出租车要多少钱？	*qù jī chǎng zuò chū zū chē yào duō shǎo qián*
To…Airport, please.	请带我去…机场。	*qǐng dài wǒ qù…jī chǎng*
My airline is…	我的航空公司是…	*wǒ de háng kōng gōng sī shì…*
My flight leaves at…	我的航班…起飞	*wǒ de háng bān…qǐ fēi*
I'm in a rush.	我在赶时间。	*wǒ zài gǎn shí jiān*
Can you take an alternate route?	你能走另一条路线吗？	*nǐ néng zǒu lìng yì tiáo lù xiàn ma*
Can you drive faster/slower?	你能开快一点/慢一点吗？	*nǐ néng kāi kuài yì diǎn/màn yì diǎn ma*

For Time, see page 163.

YOU MAY HEAR…

您乘坐哪家航空公司的班机？ *nín chéng zuò nǎ jiā háng kōng gōng sī de bān jī*	What airline are you flying?
国内还是国际航班？ *guó nèi hái shì guó jì háng bān*	Domestic or international?
哪一个候机厅 *nǎ yí gè hòu jī tīng*	What terminal?

In addition to China Airlines, many U.S. and U.K. airlines have frequent flights to China. Main cities, such as Beijing, Shanghai, Shenzhen, Guangzhou, Tianjin, Chongqing and Xi'an have international airports with flights to and from the U.S. and U.K. The procedure for departure and arrivals is similar to that at an airport in the U.S. and U.K. Duty free stores as well as transportation from the airport to the downtown area are available at most international Chinese airports.

If you plan to travel throughout China, it is a good idea to make arrangements in advance. There are a few main tourist information offices that can help you to book tickets, hotels and flights, including: China International Travel Service (www.cits.net), China Travel Service (www.chinatravelservice.com) and China Youth Travel Sevice (www.chinayouthtravel.com). Keep in mind that reservations often need to be made well in advance.

YOU MAY SEE...

抵达 *dǐ dá*	arrivals
离境 *lí jìng*	departures
认领行李 *rèn lǐng xíng li*	baggage claim
安检 *ān jiǎn*	security
国内航班 *guó nèi háng bān*	domestic flights
国际航班 *guó jì háng bān*	international flights
办理登机手续 *bàn lǐ dēng jī shǒu xù*	check-in
办理电子票登机手续	e-ticket check-in
bàn lǐ diàn zǐ piào dēng jī shǒu xù	
登机口 *dēng jī kǒu*	departure gates

Checking In

Where's check in?	在哪里办理登机手续？ *zài nǎ li bàn lǐ dēng jī shǒu xù*
My name is...	我叫… *wǒ jiào...*
I'm going to...	我要去… *wǒ yào qù...*
I have...	我有… *wǒ yǒu...*
one suitcase	一个行李箱 *yí ge xíng li xiāng*
two suitcases	两个行李箱 *liǎng ge xíng li xiāng*
one carry-on [piece of hand luggage]	一件随身行李 *yí jiàn suí shēn xíng li*
How much luggage is allowed?	允许带几件行李？ *yǔn xǔ dài jǐ jiàn xíng li*
Is that pounds or kilos?	你是指磅还是公斤？ *nǐ shì zhǐ bàng hái shì gōng jīn*
Which terminal/gate?	哪个候机厅/登机门？ *nǎ gè hòu jī tīng/ dēng jī mén*
I'd like a window/an aisle seat.	我想要靠窗口/过道的座位。*wǒ xiǎng yào kào chuāng kǒu/guò dào de zuò wèi*

When do we leave/arrive?	我们几点离开/到达？ *wǒ men jǐ diǎn lí kāi/dào dá*
Is the flight delayed?	飞机晚点了吗？ *fēi jī wǎn diǎn le ma*
How late?	有多晚？ *yǒu duō wǎn*

YOU MAY HEAR...

下一个！ *xià yí gè*	Next!
请出示护照/机票。 *qǐng chū shì hù zhào/jī piào*	Your passport/ticket, please.
您需要托运行李吗？ *nín xū yào tuō yùn xíng li ma*	Are you checking any luggage?
那件随身行李太大。 *nà jiàn suí shēn xíng li tài dà*	That's too large for a carry on [to carry on board].
您是自己打的包吗？ *nín shì zì jǐ dǎ de bāo ma*	Did you pack these bags yourself?
有人让您带东西了吗 *yǒu rén ràng nín dài dōng xi le ma*	Did anyone give you anything to carry?
掏空您的口袋。 *tāo kōng nín de kǒu dài*	Empty your pockets.
请脱鞋。 *qǐng tuō xié*	Take off your shoes.
现在…登机。 *xiàn zài...dēng jī*	Now boarding...

Luggage

Where is/are...?	…在哪里？ *...zài nǎ li*
the luggage carts [trolleys]	手推车 *shǒu tuī chē*
the luggage lockers	行李暂存箱 *xíng li zàn cún xiāng*
the baggage claim	认领行李 *rèn lǐng xíng li*

| My luggage has been lost/stolen. | 我的行李丢了/被偷了。 *wǒ de xíng li diū le/ bèi tōu le* |
| My suitcase is damaged. | 我的手提箱被损坏了。 *wǒ de shǒu tí xiāng bèi sǔn huài le* |

For Grammar, see page 156.

Throughout this phrase book, the pronoun 我 **(wǒ)** (I) is used for simplicity. However, if you are traveling with someone, use 我们 **(wǒ men)** (we).
Example:
我要买票。 **(wǒ yào mǎi piào)** I need a ticket.
我们要买票。 **(wǒ men yào mǎi piào)** We need tickets.

Finding your Way

Where is/are…?	…在哪里？ *…zài nǎ li*
the currency exchange	货币兑换 *huò bì duì huàn*
the car hire	租车 *zū chē*
the exit	出口 *chū kǒu*
the taxis	出租车 *chū zū chē*
Is there a…into town?	有没有去城里的…？ *yǒu mei yǒu qù chéng lǐ de…*
bus	公共汽车 *gōng gòng qì chē*
train	火车 *huǒ chē*
subway	地铁 *dì tiě*

For Asking Directions, see page 37.

Train

Where's the train station?	火车站在哪里？ *huǒ chē zhàn zài nǎ li*
How far is it?	有多远？ *yǒu duō yuǎn*
Where is/are…?	…在哪里？ *…zài nǎ li*
the ticket office	售票处 *shòu piào chù*
the information desk	问讯处 *wèn xùn chù*
the luggage lockers	行李暂存箱 *xíng li zàn cún xiāng*
the platforms	站台 *zhàn tái*
Can I have a schedule [timetable]?	给我一张时间表好吗？ *gěi wǒ yì zhāng shí jiān biǎo hǎo ma*
Is it a direct train?	是直达列车吗？ *shì zhí dá liè chē ma*
Do I have to change trains?	我要转车吗？ *wǒ yào zhuǎn chē ma*
How long is the trip?	旅途多长时间？ *lǚ tú duō cháng shí jiān*
Is the train on time?	火车准时吗？ *huǒ chē zhǔn shí ma*

For Asking Directions, see page 37.

For Tickets, see page 21.

YOU MAY SEE…

站台 *zhàn tái*	platforms
信息 *xìn xī*	information
预定 *yù dìng*	reservations
候车室 *hòu chē shì*	waiting room
抵达 *dǐ dá*	arrivals
离开 *lí kāi*	departures

China has a vast rail network and you can travel by train to almost every Chinese city and town. There are different types of train service available: express, 快车 **kuài chē**; regular, 慢车 **màn chē**; and non stop, 直达 **zhí dá**. For seats, there are five classes: hard seat, soft seat, hard sleeper, soft sleeper and standing. Buy a ticket at the train station or from one of the ticket offices located throughout major cities. Before boarding, have your ticket validated by an attendant at the station. In large cities, stations may have machines to validate your tickets.

Departures

Which track [platform] to…?	哪个站台去…？ *nǎ ge zhàn tái qù…*
Is this the track [platform]/train to…?	这是去…的站台/火车吗？ *zhè shì qù…de zhàn tái/huǒ chē ma*
Where is track [platform]…?	…站台在哪里？ *…zhàn tái zài nǎ li*
Where do I change for…?	我怎么转车去…？ *wǒ zěn me zhuǎn chē qù…*

On Board

Can I sit here/open the window?	我可以坐在这里/打开窗子吗？ *wǒ kě yǐ zuò zài zhè li/dǎ kāi chuāng zi ma*
That's my seat.	那是我的座位。 *nà shì wǒ de zuò wèi*
Here's my reservation.	我预订了这个座位。 *wǒ yù dìng le zhè ge zuò wèi*

YOU MAY HEAR...

请大家上车！ *qǐng dà jiā shàng chē*
请出示车票。 *qǐng chū shì chē piào*
您必须在北京换车。 *nín bì xū zài běijīng huàn chē*
下一站是上海。 *xià yí zhàn shì shàng hǎi*

All aboard!
Tickets, please.
You have to change at at Beijing.

Next stop, Shanghai.

Bus

Where's the bus station?	汽车站在哪里？ *qì chē zhàn zài nǎ li*
How far is it?	有多远？ *yǒu duō yuǎn*
How do I get to…?	我怎么去…？ *wǒ zěn me qù…*
Is this the bus to…?	这是去…的公共汽车吗？ *zhè shì qù… de gōng gòng qì chē ma*
Can you tell me when to get off?	你能告诉我什么时候下车吗？ *nǐ néng gào sù wǒ shén me shí hòu xià chē ma*
Do I have to change buses?	我要换公共汽车吗？ *wǒ yào huàn gōng gòng qì chē ma*
How many stops to…?	到…有几站？ *dào… yǒu jǐ zhàn*
Stop here, please!	请在这里停下！ *qǐng zài zhè li tíng xià*

For Tickets, see page 21.

YOU MAY SEE...

公共汽车站 *gōng gòng qì chē zhàn*
上车/下车 *shàng chē/xià chē*

bus stop
enter/exit

There are three kinds of bus systems in China: public buses for city transportation, tourist buses for sightseeing and long-distance buses for travel outside of town. Most buses run from 6:00 a.m. to 11:00 p.m. In major cities, you can purchase a monthly discounted pass for public buses. Tourist buses, which are available in major cities, may offer flexible fares (especially for groups) so be sure to negotiate with the driver. Long distance buses in China service practically every small town, including those in remote regions not accessible by train or plane. There is a bus station in almost every town, big and small, where you can find information on schedules, fares and routes. For public and long distance buses, buy your ticket at the bus station and have it validated by an attendant before boarding.

Subway

Where's the subway station?	地铁站在哪里？ dì tiě zhàn zài nǎ li
A map, please.	请给我一张地图。 qǐng gěi wǒ yì zhāng dì tú
Which line for…?	哪条线去…？ nǎ tiáo xiàn qù…
Which direction?	哪个方向？ nǎ ge fāng xiàng
Do I have to transfer [change]?	我要换地铁吗？ wǒ yào huàn dì tiě ma
Is this the subway [train] to…?	这趟地铁去…吗？ zhè tàng dì tiě qù…ma
How many stops to…?	到…有几站？ dào…yǒu jǐ zhàn
Where are we?	我们在哪里？ wǒ men zài nǎ li

For Tickets, see page 21.

Major cities in China — Beijing, Shanghai, Nanjing, Guangzhou, Shenzhen and Tianjin — have subway systems. Purchase one trip tickets and discounted montly passes at subway stations; some cities may also offer daily and/or weekend tickets. Request operation times, routes, fares, and other subway information from the ticket booth attendant. At some stations, you simply pay and enter; at others, you buy a ticket at the booth and have the ticket validated by an attendant before boarding. In large cities, stations may have machines to validate your tickets. Maps are available at the ticket booth, usually for a fee.

Boat & Ferry

When is the ferry to…?	去…的轮渡是什么时间？ *qù…de lún dù shì shén me shí jiān*
Where are the life jackets?	救生衣在哪里？ *jiù shēng yī zài nǎ li*
What time is the next sailing?	下一个航班是什么时间？ *xià yī ge háng bān shì shén me shí jiān*
Can I book a seat/cabin?	我可以预定一个座位/船舱吗？ *wǒ kě yǐ yù dìng yī gè zuò wèi/chuán cāng ma*
How long is the crossing?	横渡要多长时间？ *héng dù yào duō cháng shí jiān*

YOU MAY SEE...

救生船 jiù shēng chuán	life boat
救生衣 jiù shēng yī	life jacket

There is regular ferry and boat service between large coastal cities of China as well as along rivers, particularly the Chang Jiang (Yangzi) and Zhu Jiang (Pearl), but not the Huang He (Yellow). Some islands in Zhejiang, Fujian, Shandong, Guangdong and Liaoning are accessible by ferry. Check with a travel agent or the local ferry terminal for schedules, routes and fares.

Taxi

Where can I get a taxi?	我可以在哪里叫出租车？	*wǒ kě yǐ zài nǎ li jiào chū zū chē*
Can you send a taxi?	你们能派一辆出租车吗？	*nǐ men néng pài yī liàng chū zū chē ma*
Do you have the number for a taxi?	你有出租车公司的电话吗？	*nǐ yǒu chū zū chē gōng sī de diàn huà ma*
I'd like a taxi now/for tomorrow at...	我现在/明天想叫出租车	*wǒ xiàn zài/míng tiān xiǎng jiào chū zū chē*
Pick me up at...	在···接我	*zài...jiē wǒ*
I'm going to...	我要去···	*wǒ yào qù...*
this address	这个地址	*zhè ge dì zhǐ*
the airport	机场	*jī chǎng*
the train [railway] station	火车站	*huǒ chē zhàn*

YOU MAY HEAR...

去哪里？ *qù nǎ li*	Where to?
地址是什么？ *dì zhǐ shì shén me*	What's the address?
有夜间/机场费。 *yǒu yè jiān/jī chǎng fèi*	There's a nighttime/ airport surcharge.

I'm late.	我晚了。 *wǒ wǎn le*
Can you drive faster/slower?	你能开快/慢点吗？ *nǐ néng kāi kuài/màn diǎn ma*
Stop/Wait here.	在这里停车/等我。 *zài zhè lǐ tíng chē/děng wǒ*
How much?	多少钱？ *duō shǎo qián*
You said it would cost...	你说过要··· *nǐ shuō guò yào...*
Keep the change.	不用找零了。 *bú yòng zhǎo líng le*

Taxi service in cities is usually meter-based; in smaller towns or in the countryside, you may need to negotiate a flat fee with the driver. Hail a taxi on the street by raising your arm or grab a taxi at taxi stands, located throughout major cities and recognizable by a TAXI sign. There is usually no surcharge for luggage, but a nighttime surcharge may apply. Tipping the taxi driver is not a norm in China, but will be happily accepted.

Bicycle & Motorbike

I'd like to rent [hire]...	我想租··· *wǒ xiǎng zū...*
a bicycle	一辆自行车 *yí liàng zì xíng chē*
a moped	电动自行车 *diàn dòng zì xíng chē*
a motorcycle	一辆摩托车 *yí liàng mó tuō chē*
How much per day/week?	一天/星期多少钱？ *yì tiān/xīng qi duō shǎo qián*
Can I have a helmet/lock?	我可以买一顶头盔/一把锁吗？ *wǒ kě yǐ mǎi yì dǐng tóu kuī/yì bǎ suǒ ma*

Cycling is a popular method of transportation throughout China. Bicycles can be rented in many Chinese towns, either at hotels or bicycle shops. To avoid parking fines and to minimize the risk of having the bicycle stolen, park the bicycle at guarded parking spaces for a small fee.

Car Hire

Where's the car rental [hire]?	租车在哪里？	*zū chē zài nǎ li*
I'd like…	我想要…	*wǒ xiǎng yào…*
a cheap/small car	一辆便宜的/小一点的汽车	*yí liàng pián yi de/xiǎo yì diǎn de qì chē*
an automatic/ a manual	手动/自动	*shǒu dòng/zì dòng*
air conditioning	空调	*kōng tiáo*
a car seat	儿童安全座	*ér tóng ān quán zuò*
How much…?	…多少钱？	*…duō shǎo qián*
per day/week	每天/星期	*měi tiān/xīng qī*
per kilometer	每公里	*měi gōng lǐ*
for unlimited mileage	不限里程	*bú xiàn lǐ chéng*
with insurance	有保险	*yǒu bǎo xiǎn*
Are there any discounts?	打折吗？	*dǎ zhé ma*
Where's the parking meter?	停车计时器在哪里？	*tíng chē jì shí qì zài nǎ li*
Where's the parking garage?	车库在哪里？	*chē kù zài nǎ li*

YOU MAY HEAR...

您有国际驾照吗？ *nín yǒu guó jì jià zhào ma*

请出示您的护照。 *qǐng chū shì nín de hù zhào*

您想要保险吗？ *nín xiǎng yào bǎo xiǎn ma*

我需要押金。 *wǒ xū yào yā jīn*
在这里签上您的名字首 字母/名字。 *zài zhè li qiān shàng nín de míng zi shǒu zì mǔ/míng zi*

Do you have an international driver's license?
Your passport, please.

Do you want insurance?

I'll need a deposit.
Initial/Sign here.

Car hire agencies are available only in major cities for driving within the city limits. You can, however, hire a driver for a few hours, a day or longer at a rate that you can negotiate. Talk to your hotel concierge about safe rental options.

Fuel Station

Where's the gas [petrol] station?	加油站在哪里？ *jiā yóu zhàn zài nǎ li*
Fill it up.	请加满。 *qǐng jiā mǎn*
I'll pay in cash/by credit card.	我用现金/信用卡付款。 *wǒ yòng xiàn jīn/xìn yòng kǎ fù kuǎn*

For Numbers, see page 160.

YOU MAY SEE...

汽油	*qì yóu*	gas [petrol]
有铅	*yǒu qiān*	leaded
无铅	*wú qiān*	unleaded
普通	*pǔ tōng*	regular
超级	*chāo jí*	super
优质	*yōu zhì*	premium
柴油	*chái yóu*	diesel
自助服务	*zì zhù fú wù*	self-service
全面服务	*quán miàn fú wù*	full service

Asking Directions

Is this the way to…?	这是去···的路吗？ *zhè shì qù…de lù ma*
How far is it to…?	去···有多远 *qù…yǒu duō yuǎn*
Where's…?	···在哪里？ *…zài nǎ li*
…Street	···街 *…jiē*
this address	这个地址 *zhè ge dì zhǐ*
the highway [motorway]	高速公路 *gāo sù gōng lù*
Can you show me on the map?	你能在地图上指给我看吗？ *nǐ néng zài dì tú shàng zhǐ gěi wǒ kàn ma*
I'm lost.	我迷路了 *wǒ mí lù le*

YOU MAY HEAR...

一直向前 *yì zhí xiàng qián*	straight ahead
左边 *zuǒ biān*	left
右边 *yòu biān*	right
在/转过街角 *zài/zhuǎn guò jiē jiǎo*	on/around the corner
对面 *duì mian*	opposite
后面 *hòu mian*	behind
旁边 *páng biān*	next to
后 *hòu*	after
北/南 *běi/nán*	north/south
东/西 *dōng/xī*	east/west
在红绿灯那儿 *zài hóng lǜ dēng nà er*	at the traffic light
在十字路口 *zài shí zì lù kǒu*	at the intersection

YOU MAY SEE…

入口/出口 *rù kǒu/chū kǒu*	entrance/exit
慢 *màn*	slow
停 *tíng*	yield

Parking

Can I park here?	我可以停在这里吗？ *wǒ kě yǐ tíng zài zhè li ma*
Where's the…?	…在哪里？ *…zài nǎ li*
parking garage	车库 *chē kù*
parking lot [car park]	停车场 *tíng chē chǎng*
parking meter	停车计时器 *tíng chē jì shí qì*
How much…?	多少钱…？ *duō shǎo qián…*
per hour	每小时 *měi xiǎo shí*
per day	每天 *měi tiān*
overnight	通宵 *tōng xiāo*

Breakdown & Repair

My car broke down/ won't start.	我的汽车坏了/不启动。 *wǒ de qì chē huài le/bú qǐ dòng*
I have a puncture/ flat tyre	我的轮胎扎破了/没气了 *wǒ de lún tāi zhā pò le/méi qì le*
Can you fix it?	你能修好吗？ *nǐ néng xiū hǎo ma*
When will it be ready?	什么时候能修好？ *shén me shí hou néng xiū hǎo*
How much?	多少钱？ *duō shǎo qián*

Accidents

There was an accident	出事故了。 *chū shì gù le*
Call an ambulance/ the police.	打电话叫一辆救护车/警察。 *dǎ diàn huà jiào yí liàng jiù hù chē/jǐng chá*

Places to Stay

ESSENTIAL

Can you recommend a hotel?	你能推荐一家旅馆吗？ *nǐ néng tuī jiàn yì jiā lǚ guǎn ma*
I have a reservation.	我有预定。 *wǒ yǒu yù dìng*
My name is...	我的名字是··· *wǒ de míng zi shì...*
Do you have a room...?	有···的房间吗？ *yǒu...de fáng jiān ma*
for one/two	一/两人 *yì/liǎng rén*
with a bathroom	带浴室 *dài yù shì*
with air conditioning	带空调 *dài kōng tiáo*
For...	住··· *zhù...*
tonight	今天晚上 *jīn tiān wǎn shang*
two nights	两个晚上 *liǎng gè wǎn shang*
one week	一个星期 *yí gè xīng qī*
How much?	多少钱？ *duō shǎo qián*
Is there anything cheaper?	有没有更便宜的？ *yǒu mei yǒu gèng pián yi de*
When's check-out?	几点退房？ *jí diǎn tuì fáng*
Can I leave this in the safe?	我可以把这个留在保险柜吗？ *wǒ kě yǐ bǎ zhè ge liú zài bǎo xiǎn guì ma*
Can I leave my bags?	我可以把包留下吗？ *wǒ kě yǐ bǎ bāo liú xià ma*
Can I have my bill/ a receipt?	可以给我账单/收据吗？ *kě yǐ gěi wǒ zhàng dān/shōu jù ma*
I'll pay in cash/by credit card.	我用现金/信用卡付款。 *wǒ yòng xiàn jīn/xìn yòng kǎ fù kuǎn*

Hotels, 旅馆 **lǚ guǎn**, in China range from budget to luxury. Many quality hotels belong to international hotel chains with service and prices to match. Larger hotels may feature an English-speaking service attendant who holds room keys; handles laundry; sells cigarettes, snacks, drinks and postcards and offers general assistance. Postal, phone and foreign exchange services are usually located on the first floor.

In general, hotels are ranked from three to five stars; the majority of hotels charge a 10-15% service fee. Be sure to reserve accommodations in advance, especially if you plan to visit China during the main tourist seasons: May, September and October.

Worth mentioning are the famous, well-preserved hotels dating from colonial times: Peace Hotel, Shanghai; Grand Hotel, Beijing and People's Hotel, Xi'an. Reservations for these must be made well in advance.

Somewhere to Stay

Can you recommend…?	你能推荐…吗？ *nǐ néng tuī jiàn…ma*
a hotel	一家旅馆 *yì jiā lǚ guǎn*
a hostel	一间旅舍 *yì jiān lǚ shè*
a campsite	一个露营地 *yí gè lù yíng dì*
a bed and breakfast	一家带早餐的旅店 *yì jiā dài zǎo cān de lǚ diàn*
What is it near?	它离哪里近？ *tā lí nǎ li jìn*
How do I get there?	我怎么去那里呢？ *wǒ zěn me qù nà li ne*

At the Hotel

I have a reservation.	我有预定。 *wǒ yǒu yù dìng*
My name is…	我的名字是… *wǒ de míng zi shì*
Do you have a room…?	有…的房间吗？ *yǒu…de fáng jiān ma*
with a bathroom [toilet]/shower	带浴室/淋浴 *dài yù shì/lín yù*
with air conditioning	带空调 *dài kōng tiáo*
that's smoking/non-smoking	那是吸烟/非吸烟房间 *nà shì xī yān/fēi xī yān fáng jiān*
For…	住… *zhù…*
tonight	今晚 *jīn wǎn*
two nights	两个晚上 *liǎng gè wǎn shang*
a week	一个星期 *yí gè xīng qī*
Do you have…?	你有…吗？ *nǐ yǒu…ma*
a computer	电脑 *diàn nǎo*
an elevator [a lift]	电梯 *diàn tī*
(wireless) internet service	（无线）互联网服务 *(wú xiàn) hù lián wǎng fú wù*

room service	客房送餐服务	kè fáng sòng cān fú wù
a TV	电视机	diàn shì jī
a pool	游泳池	yóu yǒng chí
a gym	健身房	jiàn shēn fáng
I need...	我需要···	wǒ xū yào...
an extra bed	加床	jiā chuáng
a cot	一张儿童床	yì zhāng ér tóng chuáng
a crib	一个摇篮	yí gè yáo lán

For Numbers, see page 160.

YOU MAY HEAR...

请出示您的护照/信用卡。
qǐng chū shì nín de hù zhào/xìn yòng kǎ
填好这份表格。 tián hǎo zhè fèn biǎo gé
在这里签名。 zài zhè li qiān míng

Your passport/credit card, please.
Fill out this form.

Sign here.

Price

How much per night/week?	每晚/星期多少钱？	měi wǎn/xīng qī duō shǎo qián
Does that include breakfast/sales tax [VAT]?	包括早餐/销售税吗？	bāo kuò zǎo cān/xiāo shòu shuì ma
Are there any discounts?	有折扣吗？	yǒu zhé kòu ma

Preferences

Can I see the room?	我能看看房间吗？	wǒ néng kàn kan fáng jiān ma

43

I'd like a…room.	我想要一个…的房间。 *wǒ xiǎng yào yí*
	gè…de fáng jiān
better	更好 *gèng hǎo*
bigger	更大 *gèng dà*
cheaper	更便宜 *gèng pián yi*
quieter	更安静 *gèng ān jìng*
I'll take it.	我要这个房间。 *wǒ yào zhè ge fáng jiān*
No, I won't take it.	不，我不要这个房间。 *bù wǒ bú yào*
	zhè ge fáng jiān

Questions

Where's the…?	…在哪里？ *…zài nǎ li*
bar	酒吧 *jiǔ bā*
bathroom [toilet]	浴室 *yù shì*
elevator [lift]	电梯 *diàn tī*
Can I have…?	我可以要…吗？ *wǒ kě yǐ yào…ma*
a blanket	一条毯子 *yì tiáo tǎn zi*
an iron	一个熨斗 *yí gè yùn dǒu*
the room key/	房间钥匙/钥匙卡 *fáng jiān yào shi/*
key card	*yào shi kǎ*
a pillow	一个枕头 *yí gè zhěn tou*
soap	一块肥皂 *yí kuài féi zào*
toilet paper	卫生纸 *wèi shēng zhǐ*
a towel	一条毛巾 *yì tiáo máo jīn*
Do you have an	你有这个的变压器吗？ *nǐ yǒu zhè ge de*
adapter for this?	*biàn yā qì ma*
How do I turn on the	我怎么开灯？ *wǒ zěn me kāi dēng*
lights?	
Can you wake me	你能在…叫醒我吗？ *nǐ néng zài…jiào*
at…?	*xǐng wǒ ma*

The voltage used in China is 220. You may need an adapter for any appliances and electronics brought into China.

Can I leave this in the safe?	我可以把这个留在保险柜吗？	*wǒ kě yǐ bǎ zhè ge liú zài bǎo xiān guì ma*
Can I have my things from the safe?	我可以从保险柜取我的东西吗？	*wǒ kě yǐ cóng bǎo xiān guì qǔ wǒ de dōng xi ma*
Is there mail [post]/ a message for me?	有没有给我的邮件/留言？	*yǒu mei yǒu gěi wǒ de yóu jiàn/liú yán*
What time do you lock up?	几点锁门？	*jǐ diǎn suǒ mén*
Do you have a laundry service?	你们提供洗衣服务吗？	*nǐ men tí gōng xǐ yī fú wù ma*

YOU MAY SEE...

推/拉 *tuī/lā*	push/pull
浴室 *yù shì*	bathroom [toilet]
淋浴 *lín yù*	shower
电梯 *diàn tī*	elevator [lift]
楼梯 *lóu tī*	stairs
制冰机 *zhì bīng jī*	ice machines
自动售货机 *zì dòng shòu huò jī*	vending machines
洗衣 *xǐ yī*	laundry
请勿打扰 *qǐng wù dǎ rǎo*	do not disturb
防火门 *fáng huǒ mén*	fire door
(紧急) 出口 *(jǐn jí) chū kǒu*	(emergency) exit
电话叫醒 *diàn huà jiào xǐng*	wake up call

Problems

There's a problem.	出了个问题。 *chū le gè wèn tí*
I lost my key/key card.	我把钥匙/钥匙卡弄丢了。 *wǒ bǎ yào shi/ yào shi kǎ nòng diū le*
I'm locked out of the room.	我被锁在房间外面了。 *wǒ bèi suǒ zài fáng jiān wài miàn le*
There's no hot water/toilet paper.	没有热水/卫生纸。 *méi yǒu rè shuǐ/ wèi shēng zhǐ*
The room is dirty.	房间很脏。 *fáng jiān hěn zāng*
There are bugs in the room.	房间有虫子。 *fáng jiāni yǒu chóng zi*
The...doesn't work.	···不工作。 *...bú gōng zuò*
Can you fix the...?	你能修修···吗？ *nǐ néng xiū xiu...ma*
air conditioning	空调 *kōng tiáo*
fan	风扇 *fēng shàn*
heat [heating]	暖气 *nuǎn qì*
light	电灯 *diàn dēng*
TV	电视 *diàn shì*
toilet	洗手间 *xǐ shǒu jiān*
I'd like another room.	我想换房。 *wǒ xiǎng huàn fáng*

Checking Out

When's check out?	几点退房？ *jǐ diǎn tuì fáng*
Can I leave my bags here until...?	我可以把包留在这里到···吗？ *wǒ kě yǐ bǎ bāo liú zài zhè li dào...ma*
Can I have an itemized bill/ a receipt?	你能给我一张详细账单/收据吗？ *nǐ néng gěi wǒ yì zhāng xiáng xì zhàng dān/shōu jù ma*
I think there's a mistake.	我认为出错了。 *wǒ rèn wéi chū cuò le*
I'll pay in cash/by credit card.	我用现金/信用卡付款。 *wǒ yòng xiàn jīn/xìn yòng kǎ fù kuǎn*

46

Renting

I reserved an apartment/a room.	我预订了一套公寓/一间房。 *wǒ yù dìng le yì tào gōng yù/yì jiān fáng*
My name is…	我的名字是… *wǒ de míng zi shì…*
Can I have the key/ key card?	能给我钥匙/钥匙卡吗？ *néng gěi wǒ yào shi/yào shi kǎ ma*
Are there…?	有没有…？ *yǒu mei yǒu…*
dishes	盘子 *pán zi*
pillows	枕头 *zhěn tou*
sheets	床单 *chuáng dān*
towels	毛巾 *máo jīn*
utensils	餐具 *cān jù*
When do I put out the trash [rubbish]/ recycling?	我什么时候倒垃圾/回收品？ *wǒ shén me shí hòu dào lā jī/huí shōu pǐn*
The…is broken.	…坏了。 *…huài le*
air conditioner	空调 *kōng tiáo*
dishwasher	洗碗机 *xǐ wǎn jī*
freezer	冰柜 *bīng guì*
microwave	微波炉 *wēi bō lú*
refrigerator	冰箱 *bīng xiāng*

| stove | 炉子 *lú zi* |
| washing machine | 洗衣机 *xǐ yī jī* |

Domestic Items

I need...	我需要… *wǒ xū yào...*
an adapter	个变压器 *yí gè biàn yā qì*
aluminum [kitchen] foil	厨房锡纸 *chú fáng xī zhǐ*
a bottle opener	瓶启子 *píng qǐ zi*
a broom	一把笤帚 *yì bǎ tiáo zhou*
a can opener	开罐器 *kāi guàn qì*
cleaning supplies	清洁用品 *qīng jié yòng pǐn*
a corkscrew	开塞钻 *kāi sāi zuàn*
detergent	洗涤剂 *xǐ dí jì*
dishwashing liquid	洗碗液 *xǐ wǎn yè*
garbage [rubbish] bags	垃圾袋 *lā jī dài*
a lightbulb	一个电灯泡 *yí gè diàn dēng pào*
matches	一些火柴 *yì xiē huǒ chái*
a mop	一把拖把 *yì bǎ tuō bǎ*
napkins	一些餐巾 *yì xiē cān jīn*
paper towels	清洁纸巾 *qīng jié zhǐ jīn*
plastic wrap [cling film]	保鲜膜 *bǎo xiān mó*
a plunger	一个下水道疏通器 *yí gè xià shuǐ dào shū tōng qì*
scissors	一把剪刀 *yì bǎ jiǎn dāo*
a vacuum cleaner	一台吸尘器 *yì tái xī chén qì*

For In the Kitchen, see page 81.

For Oven Temperature, see page 167.

At the Hostel

Is there a bed available?	有空床吗？	*yǒu kòng chuáng ma*
Can I have…?	可以给我…吗？	*kě yǐ gěi wǒ …ma*
a single/ double room	一个单人/双人间	*yí gè dān rén/ shuāng rén jiān*
a blanket	一条毯子	*yì tiáo tǎn zi*
a pillow	一个枕头	*yí gè zhěn tou*
sheets	床单	*chuáng dān*
a towel	一条毛巾	*yì tiáo máo jīn*
Do you have lockers?	有衣物柜吗？	*yǒu yī wù guì ma*
When do you lock up?	几点锁门？	*jǐ diǎn suǒ mén*
Do I need a membership card?	要会员证吗？	*yào huì yuán zhèng ma*
Here's my International Student Card.	这是我的国际学生证。	*zhè shì wǒ de guó jì xué shēng zhèng*

Hostels in China provide inexpensive accommodation options. Beds in dorm-style rooms are the least costly choice; private rooms — ranging from singles to rooms for six or more — may also be available but will usually be reserved in advance. Be prepared to pay in cash at hostels and other budget accommodations; credit cards are often not accepted, especially at locations in small towns. Hostels in China associated with Hostelling International accept online reservations; these often offer internet service, rent bicycles and more. Visit the Hostelling International website for details.

Going Camping

Can I camp here?	我可以在这里露营吗？	*wǒ kě yǐ zài zhè li lù yíng ma*
Where's the campsite?	露营地在哪里？	*lù yíng dì zài nǎ li*
What is the charge per day/week?	每天/星期多少钱？	*měi tiān/xīng qī duō shǎo qián*
Are there…?	有没有…？	*yǒu mei yǒu…*
cooking facilities	烹饪设施	*pēng rèn shè shī*
electric outlets	电源	*diàn yuán*
laundry facilities	洗衣设施	*xǐ yī shè shī*
showers	淋浴	*lín yù*
tents for rent [hire]	供出租的帐篷	*gòng chū zū de zhàng peng*

YOU MAY SEE...

饮用水 *yǐn yòng shuǐ*	drinking water
禁止野营 *jìn zhǐ yě yíng*	no camping
禁止生火/烧烤 *jìn zhǐ shēng huǒ/ shāo kǎo*	no fires/barbecues

For Domestic Items, see page 48.

For In the Kitchen, see page 81.

Camping is fairly uncommon in China; most campsites are located near a preserve or other nature attraction. Check with your travel agent or the concierge at your hotel for more information.

Communications

ESSENTIAL

Where's an internet cafe?	网吧在哪里？ *wǎng bā zài nǎ li*
Can I access the internet/check e-mail?	我能上网/查电子邮件吗？ *wǒ néng shàng wǎng/chá diàn zǐ yóu jiàn ma*
How much per (half) hour?	每(半)个小时多少钱？ *měi (bàn) gè xiǎo shí duō shǎo qián*
How do I connect/ log on?	我怎么上网/登录？ *wǒ zěn me shàng wǎng/ dēng lù*
A phone card, please.	请给我一张电话卡。 *qǐng gěi wǒ yì zhāng diàn huà kǎ*
Can I have your phone number?	可以给我你的电话号码吗？ *kě yǐ gěi wǒ nǐ de diàn huà hào mǎ ma*
Here's my number/ e-mail.	这是我的电话号码/电子邮件地址。 *zhèshì wǒ de diàn huà hào mǎ/diàn zǐ yóu jiàn dì zhǐ*
Call/E-mail me.	给我打电话/发电子邮件。 *gěi wǒ dǎ diàn huà/fā diàn zǐ yóu jiàn*
Hello. This is...	你好，这是… *nǐ hǎo, zhè shì...*
Can I speak to...?	我可以与…讲话吗？ *wǒ kě yǐ yǔ...jiǎng huà ma*
Can you repeat that?	你能再说一次吗？ *nǐ néng zài shuō yí cì ma*
I'll call back later.	我等一会再打电话。 *wǒ děng yí huì zài dǎ diàn huà*
Bye.	再见。 *zài jiàn*
Where's the post office?	邮局在哪里？ *yóu jú zài nǎ li*
I'd like to send this to...	我想把这个送到… *wǒ xiǎng bǎ zhè ge sòng dào...*

Online

Where's an internet cafe?	网吧在哪里？ *wǎng bā zài nǎ li*
Does it have wireless internet?	有无线上网吗？ *yǒu wú xiàn shàng wǎng ma*
What is the WiFi password?	**WiFi** 密码是什么？ *WiFi mì mǎ shì shén me*
Is the WiFi free?	**WiFi** 是免费的吗？ *WiFi shì miǎn fèi de ma*
Can I access Skype?	我能上**Skype**吗？ *wǒ néng shàng Skype ma*
Do you have bluetooth?	你们有蓝牙吗？ *nǐ men yǒu lán yá ma*
How do I turn the computer on/off?	怎么开/关计算机？ *zěn me kāi/guān jì suàn jī*
Can I...?	我能…吗？ *wǒ néng…ma*
access the internet	上网 *shàng wǎng*
check e-mail	查电子邮件 *chá diàn zǐ yóu jiàn*
print	打印 *dǎ yìn*
use any computer	用计算机 *yòng jì suàn jī*
Can I...?	我能…吗？ *Wǒ néng … ma*
plug in/charge my laptop/iPhone/iPad?	插入/充电手提电脑/**iPhone**/**iPad**？ *chā rù/chōng diàn shǒu tí diàn nǎo/iPhone/iPad*

How much per (half) hour?	每(半)个小时多少钱？	měi (bàn) gè xiǎo shí duō shǎo qián
How do I...?	怎么…？	zén me …
connect/ disconnect	连接/断开	lián jiē/duàn kāi
log on/log off	登录/退出	dēng lù/tuì chū
type this symbol	输入这个符号	shū rù zhè ge fú hào
What's your e-mail?	你的电子邮件地址是什么？	nǐ de diàn zǐ yóu jiàn dì zhǐ shì shén me
My e-mail is...	我的电子邮件是…	wǒ de diàn zǐ yóu jiàn shì…
Do you have a scanner?	你们有扫描仪吗？	nǐ men yǒu sǎo miáo yí ma

Social Media

Are you on Facebook/ Twitter?	您在使用**Facebook/Twitter**吗？	nín zài shǐ yòng Facebook/Twitter ma
What's your user name?	您的用户名是什么？	nín de yòng hù míng shì shén me
I'll add you as a friend.	我会加您为好友。	wǒ huì jiā nín wéi hǎo yǒu
I'll follow you on Twitter.	我会在**Twitter**上关注您。	wǒ huì zài Twitter shàng guān zhù nín
Are you following...?	您有没有关注…？	nín yǒu mei yǒu guān zhù
I'll put the pictures on Facebook/Twitter.	我会把照片放到**Facebook/Twitter**上。	wǒ huì bǎ zhào piàn fàng dào Facebook/Twitter shàng
I'll tag you in the pictures.	我会在照片里圈您。	wǒ huì zài zhào piàn lǐ quān nín

YOU MAY SEE...

关闭 *guān bì*	close
删除 *shān chú*	delete
电子邮件 *diàn zǐ yóu jiàn*	e-mail
退出 *tuì chū*	exit
帮助 *bāng zhù*	help
即时讯息 *jí shí xùn xī*	instant messenger
互联网 *hù lián wǎng*	internet
登录 *dēng lù*	login
新(信息) *xīn (xìn xī)*	new (message)
开/关 *kāi/guān*	on/off
打开 *dǎ kāi*	open
打印 *dǎ yìn*	print
保存 *bǎo cún*	save
送 *sòng*	send
用户名/密码 *yòng hù míng/mì mǎ*	username/password
无线上网 *wú xiàn shàng wǎng*	wireless internet

Internet access centers and cafes can be found in major cities in China. Many hotels offer computer and internet facilities in their business centers as well as wireless internet access in private rooms, usually for a fee.

Phone

A phone card/prepaid phone, please.	请给我一张电话卡/预付电话卡。 *qǐng gěi wǒ yì zhāng diàn huà kǎ/yù fù diàn huà kǎ*
An international phonecard for...	给…打电话的国际电话卡 *gěi…dǎ diàn huà de guó jì diàn huà kǎ*
Australia	澳洲 *ào zhōu*
Canada	加拿大 *jiā ná dà*
Ireland	爱尔兰 *ài ěr lán*
the U.K.	英国 *yīng guó*
the U.S.	美国 *měi guó*
How much?	多少钱？ *duō shǎo qián*
Can I recharge/buy minutes for this phone?	我能给这个电话再加钱/购买更多的分钟吗？ *wǒ néng gěi zhè ge diàn huà zài jiā qián/gòu mǎi gèng duō de fēn zhōng ma*
My phone doesn't work here.	我的电话在这里不能用。 *wǒ de diàn huà zài zhè li bù néng yòng*
What network are you on?	您使用什么网络？ *nín shǐ yòng shén me wǎng luò*
Is it 3G?	是3G吗？ *shì 3G ma*
I have run out of credit/minutes.	我的通话余额/通话时间快用完了。 *wǒ de tōng huà yú é/tōng huà shí jiān kuài yòng wán le*
Can I buy some credit?	我可以充值吗？ *wǒ kě yǐ chōng zhí ma*
Do you have a phone charger?	你们有手机充电器吗？ *nǐ men yǒu shǒu jī chōng diàn qì ma*
A prepaid phone, please.	请给我一部预付费电话。 *qǐng gěi wǒ yī bù yù fù fèi diàn huà*
Where's the pay phone?	公用电话在哪里？ *gōng yòng diàn huà zài nǎ li*
What's the area/country code for...?	区号/国家代码是什么？ *qū hào/guó jiā dài mǎ shì shén me*
What's the number for Information?	问讯台号码是多少？ *wèn xùn tái hào mǎ shì duō shǎo*

Public phones can be found in most cities in China but rarely in remote areas. These phones are usually coin operated; some may be designed for use with phone cards, which can be purchased from grocery stores or newsstands. For a better rate, make your international call from calling centers or stalls, available in larger cities. Avoid making international calls from hotels, where high surcharges are added. Local calls in China are often free of charge.

For national calls, dial 0 + area code + the phone number.

For calls to the U.S. or Canada, dial 00 + 1 + area code + phone number.

For calls to the U.K., dial 00 + 44 + area code + phone number.

I'd like the number for...	我想要···的号码	*wǒ xiǎng yào...de hào mǎ*
I'd like to call collect [reverse the charges].	我想打对方付费电话。	*wǒ xiǎng dǎ duì fāng fù fèi diàn huà*
Can I have your number?	你可以给我你的号码吗？	*ni kě yǐ gěi wǒ nǐ de hào mǎ ma*
Here's my number.	这是我的号码。	*zhè shì wǒ de hào mǎ*
Please call/text me.	请给我打电话/发短信。	*qǐng gěi wǒ dǎ diàn huà/fā duǎn xìn*
I'll call/text you.	我会给你打电话/发短信。	*wǒ huì gěi nǐ dǎ diàn huà/fā duǎn xìn*

For Numbers, see page 160.

Telephone Etiquette

Hello. This is…	你好。这是…	*nǐ hǎo zhè shì…*
Can I speak to…?	我可以和…讲话吗？	*wǒ kě yǐ hé…jiǎng huà ma*
Extension…	请转…	*qǐng zhuǎn…*
Speak louder/more slowly, please.	请大声/慢慢讲。	*qǐng dà shēng/màn man jiǎng*
Can you repeat that?	你能重复吗？	*nǐ néng zài shuō yí cì ma*
I'll call back later.	我等一会儿再打电话。	*wǒ děng yí huì r zài dǎ diàn huà*
Bye.	再见。	*zài jiàn*

YOU MAY HEAR…

您是哪位？ *nín shì nǎ wèi*	Who's calling?
请稍等。 *qǐng shāo děng*	Hold on.
我给您接通。 *wǒ gěi nín jiē tōng*	I'll put you through.
他 *m*/她 *f* 不在这儿/正在接另一个电话。 *tā/tā bù zài zhè er/zhèng zài jiē lìng yí gè diàn huà*	He/She is not here/on another line.
你要不要留言？ *nǐ yào bù yào liú yán*	Would you like to leave a message?
以后/十分钟以后再打。 *yǐ hòu/shí fēn zhōng yǐ hòu zài dǎ*	Call back later/in 10 minutes.
他 *m*/她 *f* 可以给你打电话吗？ *tā/tā kě yǐ gěi nǐ dǎ diàn huà ma*	Can he/she call you back?
您的号码是什么？ *nín de hào mǎ shì shén me*	What's your number?

Fax

Can I send/receive a fax here?	这里能发/接传真吗？ *zhè lǐ néng fā/jiē chuán zhēn ma*
What's the fax number?	传真号是多少？ *chuán zhēn hào shì duō shǎo*
Please fax this to…	请把这个传真给… *qǐng bǎ zhè ge chuán zhēn gěi…*

Post

Where's the post office/mailbox [postbox]?	邮局/邮箱在哪里？ *yóu jú/yóu xiāng zài nǎ li*
A stamp for this postcard/letter to…	把这张明信片/封信寄到…的邮票 *bǎ zhè zhāng míng xìn piàn/fēng xìn jì dào…de yóu piào*
How much?	多少钱？ *duō shǎo qián*
Send this package by airmail/express	…寄这个包裹用航空/用快件 *…jì zhè ge bāo guǒ yòng háng kōng/yòng kuài jiàn*
A receipt, please.	请给我收据。 *qǐng gěi wǒ shōu jù*

YOU MAY HEAR…

填好海关申报表。 *tián hǎo hǎi guān shēn bào biǎo*
价值是多少？ *jià zhí shì duō shǎo*
里面装的是什么？ *lǐ miàn zhuāng de shì shén me*

Fill out the customs declaration form.
What's the value?
What's inside?

信 筒

开箱时间
次 09:46
16

Post offices can be found throughout China. They normally provide express, registered, overnight and general mail service. Additionally, Chinese post offices feature banking services: withdrawals, money transfers and ATMs. They may also take payment on behalf of utility companies. Online postal services are available; you can mail your packages, track their status, wire money, order merchandise, pay your utility bills and subscribe to newspapers and journals. Most online postal sites are in Chinese only.

Food & Drink

Eating Out

ESSENTIAL

Can you recommend a good restaurant/bar?	你能推荐一家好餐馆/酒吧吗？	*nǐ néng tuī jiàn yì jiā hǎo cān guǎn/jiǔ bā ma*
Is there a traditional Chinese/inexpensive restaurant nearby?	附近有没有传统的中国/不贵的餐馆？	*fù jìn yǒu mei yǒu chuán tǒng de zhōng guó/bú guì de cān guǎn*
A table for…, please.	请给我…人的桌子。	*qǐng gěi wǒ…rén de zhuō zǐ*
Can we sit…?	我们可以坐在… 吗？	*wǒ men kě yǐ zuò zài…ma*
here/there	这里/那里	*zhè li/nà li*
outside	外面	*wài miàn*
in a non-smoking area	禁烟区	*jìn yān qū*
I'm waiting for someone.	我在等人。	*wǒ zài děng rén*
Where's the restroom [toilet]?	洗手间在哪里？	*xǐ shǒu jiān zài nǎ li*
A menu, please.	请给我一份菜单。	*qǐng gěi wǒ yí fèn cài dān*
What do you recommend?	你推荐什么菜呢？	*nǐ tuī jiàn shén me cài ne*
I'd like…	我想要…	*wǒ xiǎng yào…*
Some more…, please.	请再给我一些…	*qǐng zài gěi wǒ yì xiē…*
Enjoy your meal!	请享用！	*qǐng xiǎng yòng*
The check [bill], please.	请给我账单。	*qǐng gěi wǒ zhàng dān*

Is service included?	包括服务费吗？ *bāo kuò fú wù fèi ma*
Can I pay by credit card/have a receipt?	我可以用信用卡付账/要收据吗？ *wǒ kě yǐ yòng xìn yòng kǎ fù zhàng/ yào shōu jù ma*
Thank you!	谢谢！ *xiè xie*

Where to Eat

Can you recommend...?	你能推荐···吗？ *nǐ néng tuī jiàn...ma*
a restaurant	一家餐馆 *yì jiā cān guǎn*
a bar	一间酒吧 *yì jiān jiǔ bā*
a cafe	一间咖啡馆 *yì jiān kā fēi guǎn*
a fast food place	一间快餐店 *yì jiān kuài cān diàn*
a snack bar	一间小吃店 *yì jiān xiǎo chī diàn*
a teahouse	一间茶馆 *yì jiān chá guan*
a cheap restaurant	便宜的餐馆 *pián yi de cān guǎn*
an expensive restaurant	贵的餐馆 *guì de cān guǎn*
a restaurant with a good view	带景观的餐馆 *dài jǐng guān de cān guǎn*
an authentic/ a non-touristy restaurant	地道的/非旅游式餐馆 *dì dào de/fēi lǚ yóu shì cān guǎn*

Authentic Chinese food should be one of the highlights of your trip. By Chinese tradition, food should be filling and have a healing effect; a Chinese meal is based on balance. In addition to Chinese eateries, Korean and Japanese restaurants are popular, as are international fast food restaurants.

Chinese cuisine varies greatly from region to region. The main styles are:

Beijing (Northern) cuisine

Wheat, not rice, is the staple in northern China, so Beijing cuisine is comprised mainly of noodles, steamed bread and dumplings. Beijing is the place to order Peking duck: roasted, crispy skinned duck wrapped in wafer thin pancake with spring onions and sweet bean sauce.

Cantonese (Southern) cuisine

The majority of Chinese restaurants outside of China feature Cantonese style cooking, so you will likely be familiar with the dishes and flavors. Steaming and stir-frying are the signatures of Cantonese cooking; these methods preserve the food's natural colors, flavors and vitamins. Rice, steamed or stir-fried, is the traditional accompaniment to a Cantonese-style meal.

Hunan (Central) cuisine

Chili pepper is a popular spice here, as in the neighboring Sichuan region, home of Szechuan cuisine. Hunan cuisine is known for its rich sweet and sour sauces. Smoked and cured food is also popular.

Shanghai (Eastern) cuisine

Seafood and vegetable dishes abound here, since this cuisine is based around the coastal areas of Shanghai. Be sure to sample the steamed freshwater crab, honey fried eel, yellowfish and sautéed shrimp.

Szechuan (Western) cuisine

This province is well known for its hot, peppery dishes. Food is not just spicy; Szechuan cooking combines a number of flavors: bitter, sweet, tart and sour.

Reservations & Preferences

I'd like to reserve a table...	我想预订一张…的桌子	*wǒ xiǎng yù dìng yì zhāng…de zhuō zi*
for 2	两个人	*liǎng ge rén*
for this evening	今晚	*jīn wǎn*
for tomorrow at...	明天…	*míng tiān…*
A table for 2, please.	请给我一张两个人的桌子。	*qǐng gěi wǒ yì zhāng liǎng ge rén de zhuō zǐ*
Can I get a table in the shade/sun?	能给我一张阴凉处/太阳下的餐桌吗？	*néng gěi wǒ yì zhāng yīn liáng chù/tài yang xià de cān zhuō ma*
We have a reservation.	我们有预订。	*wǒ men yǒu yù dìng*
My name is...	我的名字是…	*wǒ de míng zi shì…*
Can we sit...?	我们可以坐在…吗？	*wǒ men kě yǐ zuò zài…ma*
here/there	这里/那里	*zhè li/nà li*
outside	外面	*wài miàn*
in the shade	阴凉处	*yīn liáng chù*
in the sun	太阳下	*tài yáng xià*

in a non-smoking area	禁烟区 *jìn yān qū*
by the window	靠窗口 *kào chuāng kǒu*
Where's the restroom [toilet]?	洗手间在哪里？ *xǐ shǒu jiān zài nǎ li*

YOU MAY HEAR...

你有预订吗？ *nín yǒu yù dìng ma*	Do you have a reservation?
几位？ *jǐ wèi*	How many?
吸烟区还是禁烟区？ *xī yān qū hái shi jìn yān qū*	Smoking or non-smoking?
你可以点菜了吗？ *nín kě yǐ diǎn cài le ma*	Are you ready to order?
你想吃什么呢？ *nín xiǎng chī shén me ne*	What would you like?
我推荐… *wǒ tuī jiàn…*	I recommend…
请享用。 *qǐng xiǎng yòng*	Enjoy your meal.

How to Order

Waiter/Waitress!	服务员/服务员小姐！ *fú wù yuán/fú wù yuán xiǎo jiě*
We're ready to order.	我们可以点菜了。 *wǒ men kě yǐ diǎn cài le*
The wine list, please.	请给我酒水单。 *qǐng gěi wǒ jiǔ shuǐ dān*
I'd like…	我想要… *wǒ xiǎng yào…*
a bottle of…	一瓶… *yì píng…*
a carafe of…	一小桶… *yì xiǎo tǒng…*
a glass of…	一杯… *yì bēi…*
The menu, please.	请给我菜单。 *qǐng gěi wǒ cài dān*

Do you have…?	你们是否有…? *nǐmen shì fǒu yǒu…*
a menu in English	英语菜单 *yīng yǔ cài dān*
a fixed price menu	固定价格菜单 *gù dìng jià gé cài dān*
a children's menu	儿童菜单 *ér tóng cài dān*
What do you recommend?	你推荐什么? *nǐ tuī jiàn shén me*
What's this?	这是什么? *zhè shì shén me*
What's in it?	里面是什么? *lǐ miàn shì shén me*
Is it spicy?	辣吗? *là ma*
Without…, please.	请不要放… *qǐng bú yào fàng…*
I'd like…	我想要… *wǒ xiǎng yào…*
More…, please.	请给我再来点… *qǐng gěi wǒ zài lái diǎn…*
With/Without…, please.	请加/别加… *qǐng jiā/bié jiā…*
I can't have…	我不能吃… *wǒ bù néng chī…*
It's to go [take away].	我要拿走。 *wǒ yào ná zǒu*

For Drinks, see page 82.

YOU MAY SEE…

附加费 *fù jiā fèi*	cover charge
固定价格 *gù dìng jià gé*	fixed price
菜单 *cài dān*	menu
当日菜单 *dāng rì cài dān*	menu of the day
（没有）包括服务费 *(méi yǒu) bāo kuò fú wù fèi*	service (not) included
配菜 *pèi cài*	side dishes
特色菜 *tè sè cài*	specials

66

Cooking Methods

baked	烤 *kǎo*
boiled	煮 *zhǔ*
braised	焖 *mèn*
breaded	裹面粉 *guǒ miàn fěn*
creamed	提取乳脂 *tí qǔ rǔ zhī*
diced	切成小方块 *qiē chéng xiǎo fāng kuài*
fileted	去骨切片 *qù gǔ qiē piàn*
fried	油煎 *yóu jiān*
grilled	烤 *kǎo*
poached	水煮 *shuǐ zhǔ*
roasted	烤 *kǎo*
sautéed	炒 *chǎo*
smoked	熏 *xūn*
steamed	蒸 *zhēng*
stewed	炖 *dùn*
stuffed	有馅 *yǒu xiàn*

Dietary Requirements

I'm...	我是… *wǒ shì …*
diabetic	糖尿病患者 *táng niào bìng huàn zhě*
lactose intolerant	乳糖过敏者 *rǔ táng guò mǐn zhě*
vegan	纯素主义者 *chún sù zhǔ yì zhě*
vegetarian	我吃素 *wǒ chī sù*
I'm allergic to...	我对…过敏 *wǒ duì…guò mǐn*
I can't eat...	我不能吃… *wǒ bù néng chī…*
dairy	乳制品 *rǔ zhì pǐn*
gluten	面筋 *miàn jīn*
nuts	坚果 *jiān guǒ*

pork	猪肉	*zhū ròu*
shellfish	贝类	*bèi lèi*
spicy foods	辣的	*là de*
wheat	面食	*miàn shí*

Is it halal/kosher? 是清真食品/犹太食品吗？ *shì qīng zhēn shí pǐn/yóu tài shí pǐn ma*

Do you have…? 您有...吗？ *nín yǒu ... ma*

skimmed milk	脱脂奶	*tuō zhī nǎi*
whole milk	全脂奶	*quán zhī nǎi*
soya milk	豆奶	*dòu nǎi*

Dining with Children

Do you have children's portions? 你们有儿童餐吗？ *nǐ men yǒu ér tóng cān ma*

A highchair/child's seat, please. 请给我一把高脚椅/儿童座椅。 *qǐng gěi wǒ yì bǎ gāo jiǎo yǐ/ér tong zuò yǐ*

Where can I feed/change the baby? 我可以在哪里喂婴儿/给婴儿换尿布？ *wǒ kě yǐ zài nǎ li kě yǐ wèi yīng ér/gěi yīng ér huàn niào bù*

Can you warm this? 你能把它加热吗？ *nǐ néng bǎ tā jiā rè ma*

For Traveling with Children, see page 139.

How to Complain

How much longer will our food be? 还需要多长时间给我们上菜？ *hái xū yào duō cháng shí jiān gěi wǒ men shàng cài*

We can't wait any longer. 我们不能再等了。 *wǒ men bù néng zài děng le*

We're leaving. 我们要走了。 *wǒ men yào zǒu le*

I didn't order this. 我没要这份菜。 *wǒ méi yào zhè fèn cài*

I ordered… 我要了 ··· *wǒ yào le…*

I can't eat this. 这个不能吃。 *zhè ge bù néng chī*

This is too...	这个太··· *zhè ge tài...*
cold/hot	冷/热 *lěng/rè*
salty/spicy	咸/辣 *xián/là*
tough/bland	硬/硬/没味道 *yìng/méi wèi dao*
This isn't clean/fresh.	这个不干净/新鲜。*zhè ge bù gān jìng/xīn xian*

Paying

The check [bill], please.	请给我账单。*qǐng gěi wǒ zhàng dān*
Separate checks [bills], please.	请分开结账。*qǐng fēn kāi jié zhàng*
It's all together.	一起结账。*yì qǐ jié zhàng*
Is service included?	服务费包括在内吗？*fú wù fèi bāo kuò zài nèi ma*
What's this amount for?	这是什么费用？*zhè shì shén me fèi yòng*
I didn't have that. I had...	我没吃那个。我吃的是··· *wǒ méi chī nà ge wǒ chī de shì...*
Can I have a receipt/ an itemized bill?	我能要一张发票/明细账单吗？*wǒ néng yào yì zhāng fā piào/míng xì zhàng dān ma*
That was delicious!	那个很好吃！*nà ge hěn hǎo chī*
I've already paid.	我已经付过账了。*wǒ yǐ jīng fù guò zhàng le*

Tipping is not expected in China. However, service charges may apply in some restaurants, especially those that offer private rooms. You won't see tax included on the bill; there is no sales tax in China.

Meals & Cooking

Continental breakfast is served at most hotels that cater to
Europeans and Americans. If you prefer a Chinese breakfast, your
meal will usually be comprised of rice or wheat porridge, to which
almost anything can be added, including fried dough and salted fish.
Noodle soup with pieces of pork and/or vegetables is another popular
Chinese breakfast.

Breakfast

bacon	咸肉	*xián ròu*
bread	面包	*miàn bāo*
butter	黄油	*huáng yóu*
cereal	麦片粥	*mài piàn zhōu*
cheese	乳酪	*rǔ lào*
coffee/tea…	…咖啡／茶	*…kā fēi/chá*
black	黑	*hēi*
decaf	无咖啡因的	*wú kā fēi yīn de*
with milk	加牛奶	*jiā niú nǎi*

with sugar	加糖 *jiā táng*
with artificial sweetener	加糖精（人造甜味剂） *jiā táng jīng (rén zào tián wèi jì)*
deep fried dough sticks	油条 *yóu tiáo*
egg, fried	油煎的鸡蛋 *yóu jiān de jī dàn*
egg, hard /soft boiled	煮得老/嫩的鸡蛋 *zhǔ dé lǎo/nèn de jī dàn*
egg, hard boiled in tea leaf water and other spices	茶叶蛋 *chá yè dàn*
jam/jelly	果酱/果冻 *guǒ jiàng/guǒ dòng*
…juice	…汁 *…zhī*
apple	苹果 *píng guǒ*
grapefruit	葡萄柚 *pú táo yòu*
orange	橙子 *chéng zi*
milk	牛奶 *niú nǎi*
oatmeal	燕麦粥 *yàn mài zhōu*
omelet	摊鸡蛋 *tān jī dàn*
rice porridge	粥 *zhōu*
sausage	香肠 *xiāng cháng*
sesame seed cake	芝麻烧饼 *zhī ma shāo bing*
soy milk	豆奶 *dòu nǎi*
steamed bun	馒头 *mán tou*
steamed, stuffed bun	包子 *bāo zi*
toast	吐司 *tǔ sī*
yogurt	酸奶 *suān nǎi*
water	水 *shuǐ*
I'd like…	我想要… *wǒ xiǎng yào…*
More…, please.	请给我再来点… *qǐng gěi wǒ zài lái diǎn…*

The Chinese tend to eat early. Breakfast, 早饭 **zǎo fàn**, is usually served from 6:00 to 8:00 a.m. and lunch, 中饭 **zhōng fàn**, from 11:00 a.m to 1:00 p.m. You probably won't be able to order dinner, 晚饭 **wǎn fàn**, past 8:00 p.m., except in the south, where social life continues until late in the evening. Chinese meals are enjoyed in a group. Tables often have revolving platforms so the various dishes can be shared; using chopsticks lengthens the reach.

Appetizers

chicken feet	凤爪	*feng zhǎo*
cold jellyfish in sauce	凉拌海蛰皮	*liáng bàn hǎi zhé pí*
cold stewed beef in sauce	卤牛肉	*lǔ niú ròu*
crispy vinegar cucumber	凉拌黄瓜	*liáng bàn huáng guā*
pickles	泡菜	*pào cài*
preserved egg	皮蛋	*pí dàn*
shrimp with salt and pepper	椒盐虾	*jiāo yán xiā*
sliced ham	火腿片	*huǒ tuǐ piàn*
smoked meat	熏肉	*xūn ròu*
spring roll	春卷	*chūn juǎn*
steamed dumplings	蒸饺	*zhēng jiǎo*
steamed meat bun	蒸肉包子	*zhēng ròu bāo zi*

Chinese appetizers are ordered before a meal. In many restaurants, you can order a platter of a different appetizers, which are mostly cold dishes.

Soup

...soup	···汤	... tāng
bean curd	豆腐	dòu fu
chicken	鸡	jī
corn and egg	玉米蛋	yù mǐ dàn
egg drop	蛋花	dàn huā
hot and sour	酸辣	suān là
meat, seafood and egg	三鲜	sān xiān
pork	肉丝	ròu sī
seafood	海鲜	hǎi xiān
spare rib	排骨	pái gǔ
squid	鱿鱼	yóu yú
tomato	蕃茄	fān qié
vegetable	蔬菜	shū cài

When in China, you may wish to follow Chinese etiquette. Sip your soup directly from the soup bowl or use the ceramic soup spoon provided. Elbows remain on the table and bowls are lifted off the table while enjoying the soup.

Fish & Seafood

carp	鲤鱼 *lǐ yú*
clam	蛤蜊 *gé lì*
cod	鳕鱼 *xuě yú*
crab	螃蟹 *páng xiè*
crucian carp	鲫鱼 *jì yú*
grass carp	草鱼 *cǎo yú*
halibut	大比目鱼 *dà bǐ mù yú*
hairtail	带鱼 *dài yú*
herring	鲱鱼 *fēi yú*
lobster	龙虾 *lóng xiā*
octopus	章鱼 *zhāng yú*
oyster	牡蛎 *mǔ lì*
salmon	三文鱼 *sān wén yú*
sea bass	鲈鱼 *lú yú*
shrimp	虾 *xiā*
silver carp	鲢鱼 *lián yú*
sole	板鱼 *bǎn yú*
squid	鱿鱼 *yóu yú*
swordfish	箭鱼 *jiàn yú*
trout	鳟鱼 *zūn yú*
tuna	金枪鱼 *jīn qiāng yú*
I'd like…	我想要… *wǒ xiǎng yào…*
More…, please.	请给我再来点… *qǐng gěi wǒ zài lái diǎn…*

Meat & Poultry

cured pork	咸肉 *xián ròu*
beef	牛肉 *niú ròu*
chicken	鸡肉 *jī ròu*
duck	鸭肉 *yā ròu*
ham	火腿 *huǒ tuǐ*

(pork) heart	猪心	*zhū xīn*
(pork) kidney	猪腰	*zhū yāo*
lamb	羊肉	*yáng ròu*
(pork) liver	猪肝	*zhū gān*
oxen entrails	牛杂	*niú zá*
pork	猪肉	*zhū ròu*
rabbit	兔肉	*tù ròu*
sausage	香肠	*xiāng cháng*
(pork) spare ribs	猪排	*zhū pái*
steak	牛排	*niú pái*
pork tripe	猪肚	*zhū dǔ*
veal	小牛肉	*xiǎo niú ròu*
oxen tripe	牛百叶	*niú bǎi yè*

Vegetables & Staples

asparagus	芦笋	*lú sǔn*
broccoli	绿花菜	*lǜ huā cài*
cabbage	圆白菜	*yuán bái cài*
carrot	胡萝卜	*hú luó bo*
cauliflower	花菜	*huā cài*
celery	芹菜	*qín cài*
Chinese cabbage	白菜	*bái cài*
Chinese water spinach	空心菜	*kōng xīn cài*
corn	玉米	*yù mǐ*
Chinese long bean	豇豆	*jiāng dòu*
eggplant [aubergine]	茄子	*qié zi*
garlic	蒜	*suàn*
green bean	扁豆	*biǎn dòu*
leaf mustard	芥菜	*jiè cài*
lettuce	生菜	*shēng cài*
mushroom	蘑菇	*mó gū*

nori (type of seaweed)	紫菜	*zǐ cài*
olive	橄榄	*gǎn lǎn*
scallion	大葱	*dà cōng*
noodles	面条	*miàn tiáo*
pea	豌豆	*wān dòu*
potato	土豆	*tǔ dòu*
radish	萝卜	*luó bo*
rice	(大)米饭	*(dà) mǐ fàn*
red/green pepper	红/青柿子椒	*hóng/qīng shì zi jiāo*
seaweed	海带	*hǎi dài*
soy bean	黄豆	*huáng dòu*
spinach	菠菜	*bō cài*
tofu	豆腐	*dòu fu*
tomato	蕃茄	*fān qié*
vegetable	蔬菜	*shū cài*
zucchini	绿皮西葫芦	*lǜ pí xī hú lu*

The proper way to eat a bowl of rice is to hold the bowl up with one hand and push the rice into your mouth with chopsticks. Do not stick the chopsticks upright into a bowl of rice; this is considered an ominous sign as it resembles the incense sticks burned for funerals or at shrines. When finished with your meal, rest the chopsticks across the top of the bowl.

Fruit

apple	苹果	*píng guǒ*
apricot	杏	*xìng*
banana	香蕉	*xiāng jiāo*
cherry	樱桃	*yīng tao*

Chinese dates	枣	*zǎo*
mandarin orange	橘子	*jú zi*
fruit	水果	*shuǐ guǒ*
grapefruit	葡萄柚	*pú táo yòu*
grape	葡萄	*pú tao*
crab apple	山楂	*shān zhā*
kiwi	猕猴桃	*mí hóu táo*
lychee	荔枝	*lì zhī*
lemon	柠檬	*níng méng*
lime	酸橙	*suān chéng*
mango	芒果	*máng guǒ*
longan fruit	桂圆	*guì yuán*
melon	瓜	*guā*
orange	橙子	*chéng zi*
peach	桃子	*táo zi*
pear	梨	*lí*
pineapple	菠萝	*bō luó*
plum	李子	*lǐ zi*
pomegranate	石榴	*shí liu*
red bayberry	杨梅	*yáng méi*
strawberry	草莓	*cǎo méi*

Dessert

rice pudding with sweetened bean paste, dates, raisins, lotus seed, dried longan pulp	八宝饭	*bā bǎo fàn*
mixed fruit	水果	*shuǐ guǒ*
sweetened red bean paste	红豆沙	*hóng dòu shā*
haws on sticks (fruit similar to a crab apple, sugared and eaten off skewers)	糖葫芦	*táng hú lu*
sauteed mushrooms with milk	清炒蘑菇	*qīng chǎo mó gu*
stuffed banana	夹沙香蕉	*jiá shā xiāng jiāo*
breaded and stuffed apple slices	酥炸苹果盒	*sū zhá píng guǒ hé*
apples slices with raisins	爽口苹果沙拉	*shuǎng kǒu píng guǒ shā lā*
kiwi with carrot paste	水果雪泥	*shuǐ guǒ xuě ní*
ice cream with soda	雪碧冰淇凌	*xuě bì bīng qí líng*
apple in hot toffee	拔丝苹果	*bá sī píng guǒ*
peanut cake	花生小甜饼	*huā shēng xiǎo tián bǐng*

The Chinese rarely finish a meal with dessert but, instead, have fruit. In general sweets are eaten as snacks. You can buy desserts at bakeries and teahouses; some supermarkets have a section for desserts as well.

Sauces & Condiments

hot pepper sauce	辣酱	*là jiàng*
ketchup	番茄酱	*fān qié jiàng*
mustard	芥末	*jiè mo*
pepper	胡椒调味料	*hú jiāo tiáo wèi liào*
salt	盐	*yán*

At the Market

Where are the carts [trolleys]/baskets?	推车/篮子在哪里？	*tuī chē/lán zi zài nǎ li*
Where is…?	…在哪里？	*…zài nǎ li*
I'd like some of that/this.	我想要点那个/这个。	*wǒ xiǎng yào diǎn nà ge/zhè ge*
Can I taste it?	我能尝尝吗？	*wǒ néng cháng chang ma*
I'd like…	我想要…	*wǒ xiǎng yào…*
a kilo/half kilo of…	一公斤/半公斤…	*yì gōng jīn/bàn gōng jīn …*
a liter of…	一升…	*yì shēng…*
a piece of…	一块…	*yí kuài…*
a slice of…	一片…	*yí piàn…*
More./Less.	多点。/少点。	*duō diǎn/shǎo diǎn*
How much?	多少钱？	*duō shǎo qián*
Where do I pay?	我在哪里付钱？	*wǒ zài nǎ li fù qián*
A bag, please.	请给我一个袋子。	*qǐng gěi wǒ yí gè dài zi*
I'm being helped.	有人帮我了。	*yǒu rén bāng wǒ le*

For Conversion Tables, see page 166.

YOU MAY HEAR...

我可以帮你吗？ *wǒ kě yǐ bāng nǐ ma* — Can I help you?
你想要什么？ *nǐ xiǎng yào shén me* — What would you like?
还要别的吗？ *hái yào bié de ma* — Anything else?
那是…人民币。 *nà shì…rén mín bì* — That's…Ren Min Bi.

In major cities, you'll find supermarkets selling a variety of goods, often imported, as well as food items. Most food shopping is done at local markets, where fresh meat, fish, fruit and vegetables can be found. Rice, noodles and other staples are sold at shops labelled 主食店 **zhǔ shí diàn**. Small grocery stores, called 副食店 **fù shí diàn**, sell various goods, including meat, fish, cooking spices and sauces. You may also be able to purchase cigars and liquors here.

YOU MAY SEE...

过期日 *guò qī rì* — expiration date
卡路里 *kǎ lù lǐ* — calories
无脂肪 *wú zhī fáng* — fat free
需冷藏 *xū lěng cáng* — keep refrigerated
也许含有微量… *yě xǔ hán yǒu wēi liàng…* — may contain traces of…
微波炉可用 *wēi bō lú kě yòng* — microwaveable
在…之前出售 *zài…zhī qián chū shòu* — sell by…
适合素食者 *shì hé sù shí zhě* — suitable for vegetarians

n the Kitchen

ottle opener	开瓶器	*kāi píng qì*
owl	碗	*wǎn*
an opener	开罐器	*kāi guàn qì*
eramic spoon	汤勺	*tāng sháo*
orkscrew	开塞钻	*kai sāi zuàn*
lay pot	沙锅	*shā guō*
up	杯子	*bēi zi*
ork	叉子	*chā zi*
rying pan	煎锅	*jiān guō*
lass	玻璃杯	*bō li bēi*
nife	餐刀	*cān dāo*
rater	磨碎器	*mó suìqì*
apkin	餐巾	*cān jīn*
plate	盘子	*pán zi*
pot	锅	*guō*
spatula	铲子	*chǎn zi*
spoon	勺子	*sháo zi*
steamer	蒸锅	*zhēng guō*
wok	炒锅	*chǎo guō*

Drinks

ESSENTIAL

The wine list/drink menu, please.	请给我酒水单/饮料单。	*qǐng gěi wǒ jiǔ shuǐ dān/yǐn liào dān*
What do you recommend?	你推荐什么？	*nǐ tuī jiàn shén me*
I'd like a bottle/glass of red/white wine.	我想要瓶/杯红/白葡萄酒。	*wǒ xiǎng yào píng/bēi hóng/bái pú táo jiǔ*
The house wine, please.	请给我当家酒。	*qǐng gěi wǒ dāng jiā jiǔ*
With/Without..., please.	请加/不要加···	*qǐng jiā/bù yào jiā...*
I can't have...	我不能吃···	*wǒ bù néng chī...*
Another bottle/glass, please.	请再给我一瓶/杯。	*qǐng zài gěi wǒ yì píng/bēi*
I'd like a local beer.	我想喝当地的啤酒。	*wǒ xiǎng hē dāng dì de pí jiǔ*
Can I buy you a drink?	我可以给你买饮料吗？	*wǒ kě yǐ gěi nǐ mǎi yǐn liào ma*
Cheers!	干杯！	*gān bēi*
A coffee/tea, please.	请给我一杯咖啡/茶。	*qǐng gěi wǒ yì bēi kā fēi/chá*
Black.	黑	*hēi*
With...	加···	*jiā...*
milk	牛奶	*niú nǎi*
sugar	糖	*táng*
artificial sweetener	人造甜味剂	*rén zào tián wèi jì*
A..., please.	请给我一杯···	*qǐng gěi wǒ yì bēi...*
juice	果汁	*guǒ zhī*

soda	苏打水 *sū dá shuǐ*
(sparkling/still) water	（汽/纯净）水 *(qì/chún jìng) shuǐ*
the water safe to rink?	这水可以喝吗？ *zhè shuǐ kě yǐ hē ma*

Non-alcoholic Drinks

offee	咖啡 *kā fēi*
ola	可乐 *kě lè*
ot chocolate	热巧克力 *rè qiǎo kè lì*
ice	果汁 *guǒ zhī*
..tea	…茶 *…chá*
green	绿 *lǜ*
iced	冰 *bīng*
jasmine	茉莉花 *mò lì huā*
lemon	柠檬 *níng méng*
milk	奶 *nǎi*
oolong	乌龙 *wū lóng*

Tea is the most popular beverage in China. Though teahouses are not as common as they once were, they are still an ideal location to sample the traditional drink, enjoyed without milk or sugar. In most hotel rooms are flasks with hot water and green or black teabags. Ground coffee is hard to find, though instant coffee is generally available. Do not drink water directly from the tap. Instead, try mineral water or Chinese soft drinks — generally very sweet — which are sold everywhere. Milk is hard to find; try an international supermarket if soy milk isn't an alternative for you.

milk	牛奶 *niú nǎi*
soda	苏打水 *sū dá shuǐ*
soymilk	豆奶 *dòu nǎi*
(sparkling/still) water	（汽/纯净）水 *(qì/chún jìng) shuǐ*
yogurt drink	酸奶 *suān nǎi*

YOU MAY HEAR...

我可以给你买饮料吗？ *wǒ kě yǐ gěi nǐ mǎi yǐn liào ma* — Can I get you a drink?

加牛奶还是糖？ *jiā niú nǎi hái shì táng* — With milk or sugar?

汽水还是纯净水？ *qì shuǐ hái shì chún jìng shu* — Sparkling or still water?

Aperitifs, Cocktails & Liqueurs

brandy	白兰地 *bái lán dì*
Chinese liqueurs	白酒 *bái jiǔ*
gin	杜松子酒 *dù sōng zǐ jiǔ*
rum	兰姆酒 *lán mǔ jiǔ*
scotch	苏格兰威士忌 *sū gé lán wēi shì jì*
tequila	龙舌兰酒 *long shé lán jiǔ*
vodka	伏特加 *fú tè jiā*
whisky	威士忌 *wēi shì jì*

Beer

beer	啤酒 *pí jiǔ*
bottled/draft/canned	瓶/生/罐 *píng/shēng/guàn*
dark/light	黑/淡 *hēi/dàn*
local/imported	当地/进口 *dāng dì/jìn kǒu*
Tsingtao® beer	青岛啤酒 *qīng dǎo pí jiǔ*

Wine

wine	葡萄酒	*pú tao jiǔ*
champagne	香槟	*xiāng bīn*
red/white	红葡萄酒/白葡萄酒	*hóng pú tao jiǔ/bái pú tao jiǔ*
house/table	当家酒/佐餐酒	*dāng jiā jiǔ/zuǒ cān jiǔ*
dry/sweet	干葡萄酒/甜葡萄酒	*gān pú tao jiǔ/tián pú tao jiǔ*
sparkling	汽酒	*qì jiǔ*
dessert wine	饭后甜酒	*fàn hòu tián jiǔ*

Though the Chinese are not widely known for their alcoholic drinks, there is a surprisingly large choice on offer. Wine has been made in China for thousands of years; each region has its own speciality, usually made from rice, fruit, flowers or herbs. Chinese wine is generally sweet. Tsingtao® is a popular Chinese beer, brewed from the spring water of the Laoshan mountain. You may wish to try a local beer, too; each region has its own.

Chinese liqueurs are often infused with local favorites such as bamboo leaves, chrysanthemum and cloves. Most famous spirits include: 茅台酒 **máo tái jiǔ** and 五粮液 **wǔ liáng yè**.

On the Menu

almond	杏仁	*xìng rén*
anchovy	鲥鱼	*shí yú*
aperitif	开胃酒	*kāi wèi jiǔ*
apple	苹果	*píng guǒ*
apricot	杏子	*xìng zi*

artichoke	宝塔菜 *bǎo tǎ cài*
artificial sweetener	人造甜味剂 *rén zào tián wèi jì*
	or 糖精 *táng jīng*
asparagus	芦笋 *lú sǔn*
avocado	鳄梨 *è lí*
banana	香蕉 *xiāng jiāo*
bass	鲈鱼 *lú yú*
bay leaf	月桂叶 *yuè guì yè*
bean	豆子 *dòu zi*
bean sprout	豆芽 *dòu yá*
beef	牛肉 *niú ròu*
beer	啤酒 *pí jiǔ*
beet	甜菜 *tián cài*
blood sausage	血肠 *xuě cháng*
brandy	白兰地酒 *bái lán dì jiǔ*
bread	面包 *miàn bāo*
breast (of chicken)	鸡胸肉 *jī xiōng ròu*
broth	汤 *tāng*
butter	黄油 *huáng yóu*
buttermilk	酪乳 *lào rǔ*
cabbage	圆白菜 *yuán bái cài*
cake	蛋糕 *dàn gāo*
candy [sweets]	糖果 *táng guǒ*
caramel	麦芽糖 *mài yá táng*
caraway	芷茴香 *zhǐ huí xiang*
carrot	胡萝卜 *hú luó bo*
cashew	腰果 *yāo guǒ*
cauliflower	花菜 *huā cài*
celery	芹菜 *qín cài*
cereal	麦片粥 *mài piàn zhōu*
cheese	乳酪 *rǔ lào*

cherry	樱桃 *yīng táo*
chervil	细叶芹 *xì yè qín*
chestnut	栗子 *lì zi*
chicken	鸡肉 *jī ròu*
chickpea	鹰嘴豆 *yīng zuǐ dòu*
chicory	菊苣 *jú jù*
chili pepper	辣椒 *là jiāo*
Chinese dates	枣 *zǎo*
Chinese liquor	白酒 *bái jiǔ*
chives	韭菜 *jiǔ cài*
chocolate	巧克力 *qiǎo kè lì*
chop	剁 *duò*
chopped meat	肉馅 *ròu xiàn*
cider	苹果汁 *píng guǒ zhī*
cilantro [coriander]	香菜 *xiāng cài*
cinnamon	肉桂 *ròu guì*
clam	蛤蜊 *gé li*
clove	丁香 *dīng xiāng*
coconut	椰子 *yē zi*
cod	鳕鱼 *xuě yú*
coffee	咖啡 *kā fēi*
consommé	清炖肉汤 *qīng dùn ròu tāng*
cookie [biscuit]	曲奇 *qǔ qí*
cornmeal	玉米面 *yù mǐ miàn*
crab	螃蟹 *páng xiè*
crab apple	山楂 *shān zhā*
crabmeat	蟹肉 *xiè ròu*
cracker	薄脆饼干 *báo cuì bǐng gān*
cream	奶油 *nǎi yóu*
cream, whipped	发泡奶油 *fā pào nǎi yóu*
cream cheese	乳酪 *rǔ lào*

crucian carp	鲫鱼 *jì yú*
cucumber	黄瓜 *huáng guā*
cumin	小茴香 *xiǎo huí xiang*
cured pork	咸肉 *xián ròu*
custard	蛋羹 *dàn gēng*
dessert wine	饭后甜酒 *fàn hòu tián jiǔ*
duck	鸭肉 *yā ròu*
dumpling	饺子 *jiǎo zi*
eel	鳗鱼 *màn yú*
egg	鸡蛋 *jī dàn*
eggs with Chinese chives	韭菜炒鸡蛋 *jiǔ cài chǎo jī dàn*
eggs with cucumber	黄瓜炒鸡蛋 *huáng guā chǎo jī dàn*
eggs with a mixture of chopped meat and vegetables	芙蓉蛋 *fú róng dàn*
eggs with peeled freshwater shrimp	虾仁炒鸡蛋 *xiā rén chǎo jī dàn*
pickled egg	皮蛋 *pí dàn*
steamed egg pasty	鸡蛋羹 *jī dàn gēng*
egg yolk/white	蛋黄／蛋白 *dàn huáng/bái*
eggplant [aubergine]	茄子 *qié zi*
endive	莴苣菜 *wō mǎi cài*
escarole [chicory]	苣荬菜 *jù mǎi cài*
fennel	茴香 *huí xiang*
fig	无花果 *wú huā guǒ*
fish	鱼 *yú*
French fries	炸薯条 *zhá shǔ tiáo*
fritter	油炸馅饼 *yóu zhá xiàn bǐng*
fruit	水果 *shuǐ guǒ*
game	野味 *yě wèi*

garlic	蒜 *suàn*
garlic sauce	蒜香汁 *suàn xiāng zhī*
gherkin	嫩黄瓜 *nèn huáng guā*
giblet	杂碎 *zá suì*
gin	杜松子酒 *dù sōng zǐ jiǔ*
ginger	姜 *jiāng*
goat	羊肉 *yáng ròu*
goat cheese	羊酪 *yáng lào*
goose	鹅肉 *é ròu*
gooseberry	鹅莓 *é méi*
grapefruit	柚子 *yòu zi*
grapes	葡萄 *pú táo*
grass carp	草鱼 *cǎo yú*
green bean	青豆 *qīng dòu*
guava	番石榴 *fān shí liu*
guinea fowl	珍珠鸡 *zhēn zhū jī*
haddock	黑线鳕 *hēi xiàn xuě*
hake	无须鳕 *wú xū xuě*
halibut	大比目鱼 *dà bǐ mù yú*
ham	火腿 *huǒ tuǐ*
hamburger	汉堡包 *hàn bǎo bāo*
hazelnut	榛子 *zhēn zi*
heart	心脏 *xīn zàng*
hen	母鸡 *mǔ jī*
herb	草本 *cǎo běn*
herring	鲱鱼 *fēi yú*
honey	蜂蜜 *fēng mì*
hot dog	热狗 *rè gǒu*
ice (cube)	冰 *bīng*
ice cream	冰淇凌 *bīng qi líng*
jam	果酱 *guǒ jiàng*

jelly	果冻	*guǒ dòng*
juice	果汁	*guǒ zhī*
kid	小羊肉	*xiǎo yáng ròu*
kidney	腰花	*yāo huā*
kiwi	猕猴桃	*mí hóu táo*
lamb	小羊肉	*xiǎo yáng ròu*
leek	韭葱	*jiǔ cōng*
leg	大腿肉	*dà tuǐ ròu*
lemon	柠檬	*níng méng*
lemonade	柠檬水	*níng méng shuǐ*
lentil	扁豆	*biǎn dòu*
lettuce	生菜	*shēng cài*
lime	酸橙	*suān chéng*
liver	肝脏	*gān zàng*
lobster	龙虾	*lóng xiā*
longan fruit	桂圆	*guì yuán*
loin	腰肉	*yāo ròu*
macaroni	通心粉	*tōng xīn fěn*
mackerel	鲭鱼	*qīng yú*
mandarin orange	橘子	*jú zi*
mango	芒果	*máng guǒ*
margarine	人造黄油	*rén zào huáng yóu*
marmalade	桔子酱	*jú zi jiàng*
marzipan	小杏仁饼	*xiǎo xìng rén bǐng*
mayonnaise	蛋黄酱	*dàn huáng jiàng*
meat	肉	*ròu*
melon	瓜	*guā*
meringue	蛋白甜饼	*dàn bái tián bǐng*
milk	牛奶	*niú nǎi*
milk shake	奶昔	*nǎi xī*
mint	薄荷	*bò he*

monkfish	扁鲨	*biǎn shā*
mushroom	蘑菇	*mó gu*
mussel	淡菜	*dàn cài*
mutton	羊肉	*yáng ròu*
noodle	面条	*miàn tiáo*
nori (a type of seaweed)	紫菜	*zǐ cài*
nougat	牛乳糖	*niú rǔ táng*
nutmeg	肉豆蔻	*ròu dòu kòu*
nuts	坚果	*jiān guǒ*
octopus	章鱼	*zhāng yú*
olive	橄榄	*gǎn lǎn*
olive oil	橄榄油	*gǎn lǎn yóu*
omelet	摊鸡蛋	*tān jī dàn*
onion	葱	*cōng*
orange	橙子	*chéng zi*
orange liqueur	甜橙酒	*tián chéng jiǔ*
oregano	牛至	*niú zhì*
organ meat [offal]	杂碎	*zá suì*
ox	黄牛肉	*huáng niú ròu*
oxtail	牛尾	*niú wěi*
oyster	牡蛎	*mǔ lì*
pancake	烙饼	*lào bǐng*
papaya	番木瓜	*fān mù guā*
paprika	辣椒粉	*là jiāo fěn*
pastry	酥皮点心	*sū pí diǎn xīn*
peach	桃子	*táo zi*
peanut	花生	*huā shēng*
pear	梨	*lí*
peas	豌豆	*wān dòu*
pecan	胡桃	*hú táo*
pepper (vegetable)	柿子椒	*shì zi jiāo*

pheasant	野鸡	*yě jī*
pickle	泡菜	*pào cài*
pie	馅饼	*xiàn bǐng*
pineapple	菠萝	*bō luó*
pizza	比萨饼	*bǐ sà bǐng*
plum	李子	*lǐ zi*
pomegranate	石榴	*shí liu*
pork	猪肉	*zhū ròu*
potato	土豆	*tǔ dòu*
potato chips [crisps]	薯片	*shǔ piàn*
poultry	禽肉	*qín ròu*
prune	梅干	*méi gàn*
pumpkin	南瓜	*nán guā*
quail	鹌鹑	*ān chún*
rabbit	兔子肉	*tù zi ròu*
radish	萝卜	*luó bo*
raisin	葡萄干	*pú táo gān*
red bayberry	杨梅	*yáng méi*
red cabbage	红叶卷心菜	*hóng yè juǎn xīn cài*
relish	调味品	*tiáo wèi pǐn*
rhubarb	大黄	*dà huáng*
rice	大米	*dà mǐ*
roast	烘烤	*hōng kǎo*
roast beef	烤牛肉	*kǎo niú ròu*
roll	卷	*juǎn*
rum	兰姆酒	*lán mǔ jiǔ*
salad	沙拉	*shā lā*
salami	蒜味咸腊肠	*suàn wèi xián là cháng*
salmon	三文鱼	*sān wén yú*
sandwich	三明治	*sān míng zhì*
sardine	沙丁鱼	*shā dīng yú*

sauce	调味汁 *tiáo wèi zhī*
sausage	香肠 *xiāng cháng*
scallion [spring onion]	大葱 *dà cōng*
scallop	扇贝 *shàn bèi*
scotch	苏格兰威士忌 *sū gé lán wēi shì jì*
sea bass	鲈鱼 *lú yú*
sea perch	中国花鲈 *zhōng guó huā lú*
seafood	海鲜 *hǎi xiān*
seaweed	海带 *hǎi dài*
shallot	青葱 *qīng cōng*
shank	小腿肉 *xiǎo tuǐ ròu*
shellfish	贝类 *bèi lèi*
sherry	雪利酒 *xuě lì jiǔ*
shoulder	前腿肉 *qián tuǐ ròu*
shrimp	虾 *xiā*
silver carp	鲢鱼 *lián yú*
sirloin	牛腩 *niú nán*
snack	零食 *líng shí*
snail	蜗牛 *wō niú*
soda	苏打水 *sū dá shuǐ*
sole	板鱼 *bǎn yú*
soup	汤 *tāng*
sour cream	酸奶油 *suān nǎi yóu*
soy [soya]	大豆 *dà dòu*
soy sauce	酱油 *jiàng yóu*
soybean [soya bean]	大豆 *dà dòu*
soymilk [soya milk]	豆奶 *dòu nǎi*
spaghetti	(意)细条实心面 *(Italian) xì tiáo shí xīn miàn*
spices	调料 *tiáo liào*
spinach	菠菜 *bō cài*
spirits	酒 *jiǔ*

squash	南瓜	*nán guā*
squid	乌贼	*wū zéi*
steak	牛排	*niú pái*
stewed fruit	炖果子	*dùn guǒ zi*
strawberry	草莓	*cǎo méi*
suckling pig	乳猪	*rǔ zhū*
sugar	糖	*táng*
sweets	甜点	*tián diǎn*
sweet and sour sauce	甜酸酱	*tián suān jiàng*
sweet corn	甜玉米	*tián yù mǐ*
sweet pepper	甜椒	*tián jiāo*
sweet potato	红薯	*hóng shǔ*
sweetener	糖精	*táng jīng*
swordfish	剑鱼	*jiàn yú*
syrup	糖浆	*táng jiāng*
tangerine	蜜桔	*mì jú*
tarragon	龙篙	*lóng hāo*
tea	茶	*chá*
thyme	麝香草	*shè xiang cǎo*
tofu	豆腐	*dòu fu*
breaded tofu	锅塌豆腐	*guō tā dòu fu*
cold tofu with garlic sauce	凉拌豆腐	*liáng bàn dòu fu*
crushed tofu with pickled egg	皮蛋豆腐	*pí dàn dòu fu*
fried, stuffed tofu	锅贴豆腐	*guō tiē dòu fu*
spicy tofu	麻婆豆腐	*má pó dòu fu*
sauteed tofu	熘豆腐	*liū dòu fu*
tofu in a clay pot	沙锅豆腐	*shā guō dòu fu*
tofu with fish	鱼片豆腐	*yú piàn dòu fu*
tofu with meatballs	肉丸豆腐	*ròu wán dòu fu*

ofu with peeled freshwater shimp	虾仁豆腐	*xiā rén dòu fu*
oast	烤面包	*kǎo miàn bāo*
omato	蕃茄	*fān qié*
ongue	舌头	*shé tou*
onic water	奎宁水	*kuí níng shuǐ*
ripe	肚子	*dǔ zi*
rout	鳟鱼	*zūn yú*
ruffles	块菌	*kuài jūn*
una	金枪鱼	*jīn qiāng yú*
urkey	火鸡	*huǒ jī*
urnip	白萝卜	*bái luó bo*
anilla	香草	*xiāng cǎo*
eal	小牛肉	*xiǎo niú ròu*
egetable	蔬菜	*shū cài*
enison	鹿肉	*lù ròu*
ermouth	苦艾酒	*kǔ ài jiǔ*
inegar	醋	*cù*
odka	伏特加	*fú tè jiā*
affle	奶蛋烘饼	*nǎi dàn hōng bǐng*
alnut	核桃	*hé tao*
ater	水	*shuǐ*
atercress	西洋菜	*xī yáng cài*
atermelon	西瓜	*xī guā*
heat	面粉	*miàn fěn*
hisky	威士忌	*wēi shì jì*
ine	葡萄酒	*pú táo jiǔ*
ogurt	酸奶	*suān nǎi*
ucchini [courgette]	绿皮西葫芦	*lǜ pí xī hú lu*

People

onversation

SSENTIAL

ello!	你好！	*nǐ hǎo*
ow are you?	你好吗？	*nǐ hǎo ma*
ne, thanks.	很好，谢谢。	*hěn hǎo, xiè xie*
xcuse me!	请问！	*qǐng wèn*
o you speak English?	你讲英语吗？	*nǐ jiǎng yīng yǔ ma*
hat's your name?	你叫什么名字？	*nǐ jiào shén me míng zi*
y name is…	我叫…	*wǒ jiào …*
ce to meet you.	见到你很高兴。	*jiàn dào nǐ hěn gāo xìng*
here are you from?	你从哪里来？	*nǐ cóng nǎ li lái*
m from the U.S./ K.	我从美国/英国来。	*wǒ cóng měi guó/ yīng guó lái*
hat do you do?	你做什么工作？	*nǐ zuò shén me gōng zuò*
work for…	我为…工作。	*wǒ wéi…gōng zuò*
m a student.	我是学生。	*wǒ shì xué shēng*
m retired.	我退休了。	*wǒ tuì xiū le*
o you like…?	你想…？	*nǐ xiǎng…*
oodbye.	再见。	*zài jiàn*

It is polite to address people with: Sir, 先生 (**xiān shēng**), Madam, 女士 (**nǚ shì**) or Miss, 小姐 (**xiǎo jiě**). The Chinese also give special respect to older men and women by addressing them with 大爷 (**dà ye**) and 大娘 (**dà niáng**), respectively.

Language Difficulties

Do you speak English?	你说英语吗？	*nǐ shuō yīng yǔ ma*
Does anyone here speak English?	这里有谁说英语吗？	*zhè li yǒu shéi shuō yīng yǔ ma*
I don't speak Chinese.	我不会说中文。	*wǒ bú huì shuō zhōng wén*
Can you speak more slowly?	你能说慢一点吗？	*nǐ néng shuō màn yì diǎn ma*
Can you repeat that?	你能再说一次吗？	*nǐ néng zài shuō yí cì ma*
Excuse me?	请问？	*qǐng wèn*
What was that?	那是什么？	*nà shì shén me*
Can you spell it?	你能把它拼出来吗？	*nǐ néng bǎ tā pīn chū lái ma*
Please write it down.	请把它写下来。	*qǐng bǎ tā xiě xià lái*
Can you translate this into English for me?	你能把这个翻译成英语吗？	*nǐ néng bǎ zhè ge fān yì chéng yīng yǔ ma*
What does this/that mean?	这个/那个是什么意思？	*zhè ge/nà ge shì shén me yì si*
I understand.	我明白了。	*wǒ míng bai le*
I don't understand.	我不明白。	*wǒ bù míng bai*
Do you understand?	你明白了吗？	*nǐ míng bai le ma*

YOU MAY HEAR...

我只说一点英语。 *wǒ zhǐ shuō yì diǎn yīng yǔ* — I only speak a little English.

我不会说英语。 *wǒ bú huì shuō yīng yǔ* — I don't speak English.

Making Friends

Hello!	你好！	nǐ hǎo
Good morning.	早晨好。	zǎo chén hǎo
Good afternoon.	下午好。	xià wu hǎo
Good evening.	晚上好。	wǎn shang hǎo
My name is...	我的名字是…	wǒ de míng zi shì...
What's your name?	你叫什么名字？	nǐ jiào shén me míng zi
I'd like to introduce you to...	我想向你介绍…	wǒ xiǎng xiàng nǐ jiè shào...
Pleased to meet you.	见到你很高兴。	jiàn dào nǐ hěn gāo xìng
How are you?	你好吗？	nǐ hǎo ma
Fine, thanks. And you?	很好，谢谢。你呢？	hěn hǎo xiè xie nǐ ne

A light, quick handshake is generally an accepted greeting in China. A subtle nod and slight bow are other common greetings. You may also see someone lowering his or her eyes upon meeting someone; this is a gesture of respect.

Travel Talk

I'm here...	我在这里···	wǒ zài zhè li...
on business	–出差	chū chāi
on vacation [holiday]	度假	dù jià
studying	学习	xué xí
I'm staying for...	我要呆···	wǒ yào dài...
I've been here...	我在这里已经···了	wǒ zài zhè li yǐ jīng...le
a day	一天	yì tiān
a week	一个星期	yí gè xīng qī
a month	一个月	yí gè yuè
Where are you from?	你从哪里来？	nǐ cóng nǎ li lái
I'm from...	我来自···	wǒ lái zì...
Have you ever been to...?	你去过···吗？	nǐ qù guò...ma
Australia	澳洲	ào zhōu
Canada	加拿大	jiā ná dà
Ireland	爱尔兰	ài ěr lán
the U.K.	英国	yīng guó
the U.S.	美国	měi guó

For Numbers, see page 160.

Personal

Who are you with?	你和谁一起来的？	nǐ hé shéi yì qǐ lái de
I'm here alone.	我是一个人来的。	wǒ shì yí ge rén lái de
I'm with my...	我和我的···一起来的。	wǒ hé wǒ de...yì qǐ lái de
husband/wife	丈夫/妻子	zhàng fu/qī zǐ
boyfriend/girlfriend	男/女朋友	nán/nü péng you
friend(s)/	朋友	péng yǒu

colleague(s)	同事 *tóng shì*
When's your birthday?	你的生日是什么时候？ *nǐ de shēng rì shì shén me shí hòu*
How old are you?	你多大年纪了？ *nǐ duō dà nián jì le*
I'm...	我… *wǒ...*
Are you married?	你结婚了吗？ *nǐ jié hūn le ma*
I'm...	我… *wǒ...*
single/in a relationship	单身/有固定朋友 *dān shēn/yǒu gù dìng péng you*
engaged/married	订婚/结婚了 *dìng hūn/jié hūn le*
divorced/separated	离婚/分居了 *lí hūn/fēn jū le*
widowed	我的妻子/丈夫去世了 *wǒ de qī zi / zhàng fu qù shì le*
Do you have children/ grandchildren?	你有孩子/孙子吗？ *nǐ yǒu hái zi/sūn zi ma*

For Numbers, see page 160.

Work & School

What do you do?	你做什么工作？ *nǐ zuò shén me gōng zuò*
What are you studying?	你在学什么？ *nǐ zài xué shén me*
I'm studying Chinese.	我在学中文。 *wǒ zài xué zhōng wén*
I...	我… *wǒ...*
am a consultant	是一位顾问 *shì yí wèi gù wèn*
am unemployed	失业了 *shī yè le*
work at home	在家工作 *zài jiā gōng zuò*
Who do you work for?	你为谁工作？ *nǐ wèi shéi gōng zuò*
I work for...	我为…工作。 *wǒ wèi...gōng zuò*
Here's my business card.	这是我的名片。 *zhè shì wǒ de míng piàn*

For Business Travel, see page 137.

Weather

What's the forecast?	天气预报如何？	*tiān qì yù bào rú hé*
What beautiful/ terrible weather!	今天天气真好/不好！	*jīn tiān tiān qì zhēn hǎo/bù hǎo*
It's...	今天…	*jīn tiān…*
cool/warm	凉快/暖和	*liáng kuài/nuǎn huo*
cold/hot	冷/热	*lěng/rè*
rainy/sunny	下雨/晴天	*xià yǔ/qíng tiān*
snowy/icy	下雪/有冰	*xià xuě/yǒu bīng*
Do I need a jacket/ an umbrella?	我需要外套/雨伞吗？	*wǒ xū yào wài tào/ yǔ sǎn ma*

For Temperature, see page 167.

Romance

ESSENTIAL

Would you like to go out for a drink/ dinner?	你想出去喝一杯/吃晚饭吗？	*nǐ xiǎng chū qù hē yì bēi/chī wǎn fàn ma*
What are your plans for tonight/ tomorrow?	今晚/明天你有什么计划吗？	*jīn wǎn/ míng tiān nǐ yǒu shén me jì huà ma*
Can I have your number?	可以给我你的电话号码吗？	*kě yǐ gěi wǒ nǐ de diàn huà hào mǎ ma*
Can I join you?	我可以加入吗？	*wǒ kě yǐ jiā rù ma*
Can I get you a drink?	我可以为你买杯饮料吗？	*wǒ kě yǐ wéi nǐ mǎi bēi yǐn liào ma*
I like/love you.	我喜欢/爱你。	*wǒ xǐ huan/ài nǐ*

The Dating Game

Would you like to go out for coffee?	你想出去喝咖啡吗？	*nǐ xiǎng chū qù hē kā fēi ma*
What are your plans for…?	你···有什么计划吗？	*nǐ…yǒu shén me jì huà ma*
today	今天	*jīn tiān*
tonight	今晚	*jīn wǎn*
tomorrow	明天	*míng tiān*
this weekend	这个周末	*zhè ge zhōu mò*
Where would you like to go?	你想去哪里？	*nǐ xiǎng qù nǎ lǐ*
I'd like to go to…	我想去···	*wǒ xiǎng qù…*
Do you like…?	你喜欢···吗？	*nǐ xǐ huan…ma*
Can I have your number/e-mail?	可以给我你的电话号码/电子邮件地址吗？	*kě yǐ gěi wǒ nǐ de diàn huà hào mǎ/ diàn zǐ yóu jiàn dì zhǐ ma*
Can I join you?	我可以加入吗？	*wǒ kě yǐ jiā rù ma*
You're very attractive.	你非常漂亮。	*nǐ fēi cháng piào liang*
Let's go somewhere quieter.	我们去个更安静的地方吧。	*wǒ men qù gè gèng ān jìng de dì fang ba*

For Communications, see page 51.

Accepting & Rejecting

I'd love to.	好的。 *hǎo de*
Where should we meet?	我们在哪见面？ *wǒ men zài nǎ jiàn miàn*
I'll meet you at the bar/at your hotel.	我在酒吧/你的旅馆见你。 *wǒ zài jiǔ bā/nǐ de lǚ guǎn jiàn nǐ*
I'll come by at…	我在···拜访你 *wǒ zài…bài fǎng nǐ*
What is your address?	你的地址是什么？ *nǐ de dì zhǐ shì shén me*
I'm busy.	我很忙。 *wǒ hěn máng*
I'm not interested.	我没兴趣。 *wǒ méi xìng qù*
Leave me alone.	让我自己呆一会儿。 *ràng wǒ zì jǐ dāi yí huì er*
Stop bothering me!	不要打扰我！ *bú yào dǎ rǎo wǒ*

For Time, see page 163.

Getting Intimate

Can I hug/kiss you?	我可以拥抱/吻你吗？ *wǒ kě yǐ yōng bào/wěn nǐ ma*
Yes.	行。 *xíng*
No.	不行。 *bù xíng*
I like/love you.	我喜欢/爱你。 *wǒ xǐ huan/ài nǐ*
Stop!	住手！ *zhù shǒu*

The Chinese are generally reserved and may not be comfortable when asked forward or aggressive questions regarding romance or sexuality.

Sexual Preferences

Are you gay?	你是男同性恋吗？	*nǐ shì nán tóng xìng liàn ma*
I'm…	我是···	*wǒ shì…*
heterosexual	异性恋	*yì xìng liàn*
homosexual	同性恋	*tóng xìng liàn*
bisexual	双性恋者	*shuāng xìng liàn zhě*
Do you like men/women?	你喜欢男人/女人吗？	*nǐ xǐ huan nán rén/n ˘ü rén ma*
Let's go to a gay bar/club.	我们去一家同性恋酒吧/俱乐部吧。	*wǒ men qù yì jiā tóng xìng liàn jiǔ bā/jù lè bù ba*

Chinese attitudes regarding homosexuality are conservative; therefore, asking about a person's sexuality may not be an appropriate question. Drawing attention to one's sexual orientation is generally discouraged.

The gay community in major Chinese cities is growing, though. Larger cities in China may have gay-friendly bars and clubs but often in discreet locations.

Leisure Time

Sightseeing

ESSENTIAL

Where's the tourist information office?	旅游信息办公室在哪里？	*lǚ yóu xìn xī bàn gōng shì zài nǎ li*
What are the main attractions?	主要景点是什么？	*zhǔ yào jǐng diǎn shì shén me*
Are there tours in English?	有英语导游吗？	*yǒu yīng yǔ dǎo yóu ma*
Can I have a map/guide?	我可以要一张地图/指南吗？	*wǒ kě yǐ yào yì zhāng dì tú/zhǐ nán ma*

Tourist Information

Do you have information on...?	你了解…的信息吗？	*nǐ liǎo jiě...de xìn xī ma*
Can you recommend...?	你能推荐…吗？	*nǐ néng tuī jiàn...ma*
a bus tour	公共汽车旅游	*gōng gòng qì chē lǚ yóu*
an excursion to...	去…的旅游	*qù...de lǚ yóu*
a sightseeing tour	观光旅游	*guān guāng lǚ yóu*

Visit a travel agency while in China for tourist information. Agencies that often cater to foreigners include China Travel Services (CTS) and China International Travel Service (CITS) — see page 24; the latter has branches throughout China. Such agencies offer a variety of services: arranging tours; reserving hotels and places to stay; providing tickets for trains, operas, acrobatic performances, concerts and more.
Small scale tour operators can also be of assistance; be sure that the tour operator is licensed before requesting any service.

On Tour

I'd like to go on the tour to...	我想去…旅游。 *wǒ xiǎng qù... lǚ yóu*
When's the next tour?	下次旅游是什么时候？ *xià cì lǚ yóu shì shén me shí hòu*
Are there tours in English?	有英语导游吗？ *yǒu yīng yǔ dǎo yóu ma*
Is there an English guide book/audio guide?	有英语的旅游手册/录音旅游指南吗？ *yǒu yīng yǔ de lǚ yóu shǒu cè/lù yīn lǚ yóu zhǐ nán ma*
What time do we leave/return?	我们什么时候出发/回来？ *wǒ men shén me shí hòu chū fā/huí lái*
We'd like to see...	我们想看看… *wǒ men xiǎng kàn kan...*
Can we stop here...?	我们可以停在这里…吗？ *wǒ men kě yǐ tíng zài zhè li...ma*
to take photos	照相 *zhào xiàng*
for souvenirs	买纪念品 *mǎi jì niàn pǐn*
for the restrooms [toilets]	去洗手间 *qù xǐ shǒu jiān*
Is it handicapped [disabled] accessible?	残疾人可以使用吗？ *cán jí rén kě yǐ shǐ yòng ma*

For Tickets, see page 21.

Seeing the Sights

Where is/are the...?	…在哪里？ *...zài nǎ li*
battleground	战场 *zhàn chǎng*
botanical garden	植物园 *zhí wù yuán*
city hall	市政大厅 *shì zhèng dà tīng*
downtown area	市中心 *shì zhōng xīn*
fountain	喷泉 *pēn quán*

Great Hall of the People	人民大会堂 *rén mín dà huì táng*
library	图书馆 *tú shū guǎn*
market	商场 *shāng chǎng*
(war) memorial	（战争）纪念馆 *(zhàn zhēng) jì niàn guǎn*
museum	博物馆 *bó wù guǎn*
old town	古镇 *gǔ zhèn*
opera house	歌剧院 *gē jù yuàn*
palace	宫殿 *gōng diàn*
park	公园 *gōng yuán*
ruins	遗迹 *yí jì*
shopping area	购物区 *gòu wù qū*
Can you show me on the map?	你能在地图上指给我看吗？ *nǐ néng zài dì tú shàng zhǐ gěi wǒ kàn ma*
Is it disabled accessible?	残疾人可以使用吗？ *cán jí rén kě yǐ shǐ yòng ma*
It's…	那很… *nà hěn…*
amazing	了不起 *liǎo bu qǐ*
beautiful	漂亮 *piào liang*
boring	没意思 *méi yì si*
interesting	有意思 *yǒu yì si*
magnificent	壮观 *zhuàng guān*
romantic	浪漫 *làng màn*
strange	奇怪 *qí guài*
stunning	让人震惊 *ràng rén zhèn jīng*
terrible	可怕 *kě pà*
ugly	难看 *nán kàn*
I (don't) like it.	我（不）喜欢。 *wǒ (bù) xǐ huan*

For Asking Directions, see page 37.

Sights in China not to be missed include: the Great Wall,
Imperial Palace, Summer Palace, Temple of Heaven, Ming tombs,
Xi'an terracotta warriors and much more. Temples, gardens and other
sights can be found in even the smallest towns. For local sights, check
with your hotel concierge or a nearby travel agency. Sights are often
listed on town maps, which can be purchased at newsstands and from
street vendors.

There is much to see in China and, after a day filled with sightseeing, you
may wish to enjoy quality entertainment: concerts, acrobatics, Chinese
ballet and opera. Of these, a not to be missed event is the Beijing opera, a
spectacular combination of song, dance, pantomime and martial arts.

Religious Sites

Where's the…?	…在哪里？ …zài nǎ li
Catholic/Protestant	天主教/新教徒教堂 tiān zhǔ jiào/xīn
church	jiào tú jiào táng
mosque	清真寺 qīng zhēn sì
shrine	神殿 shén diàn
synagogue	犹太教堂 yóu tài jiào táng
temple	寺庙 sì miào
What time is mass/	弥撒/礼拜是什么时候？ mí sa/lǐ bài shì
the service?	shén me shí hòu

The People's Republic of China officially subscribes to atheism
but, since China's reform, open religious activity has been
permitted. Buddhism is the most widely practiced religion in China;
Taoism, Islam and Christianity are also observed.

Shopping

ESSENTIAL

Where's the market/ mall [shopping centre]?	市场/购物中心在哪里？	*shì chăng/gòu wù zhōng xīn zài nă li*
I'm just looking.	我只是看看。	*wŏ zhĭ shì kàn kan*
Can you help me?	你能帮我吗？	*nĭ néng bāng wŏ ma*
I'm being helped.	有人帮我了。	*yŏu rén bāng wŏ le*
How much?	多少钱？	*duō shăo qián*
That one, please.	请给我那个。	*qĭng gĕi wŏ nèi ge*
That's all.	就这些。	*jiù zhè xiē*
Where can I pay?	我在哪里付款？	*wŏ zài nă li fù kuăn*
I'll pay in cash/by credit card.	我用现金/信用卡付款。	*wŏ yòng xiàn jīn/xìn yòng kă fù kuăn*
A receipt, please.	请给我收据。	*qĭng gĕi wŏ shōu jù*

At the Shops

Where's the...?	…在哪里？	*...zài nă li*
antiques store	古董店	*gŭ dŏng diàn*

bakery	面包店	*miàn bāo diàn*
bank	银行	*yín háng*
bookstore	书店	*shū diàn*
camera store	照相机商店	*zhào xiàng jī shāng diàn*
clothing store	服装店	*fú zhuāng diàn*
delicatessen	熟食店	*shú shí diàn*
department store	百货商店	*bǎi huò shāng diàn*
gift shop	礼品店	*lǐ pǐn diàn*
health food store	健康食品店	*jiàn kāng shí pǐn diàn*
jeweler	珠宝店	*zhū bǎo diàn*
liquor store [off licence]	酒店	*jiǔ diàn*
food market	食品市场	*shí pǐn shì chǎng*
music store	音乐商店	*yīn yuè shāng diàn*
pastry shop	面包点心店	*miàn bāo diǎn xīn diàn*
pharmacy [chemist]	药房	*yào fáng*
produce [grocery] store	食品店	*shí pǐn diàn*
shoe store	鞋店	*xié diàn*
shopping mall [shopping centre]	购物中心	*gòu wù zhōng xīn*
souvenir store	纪念品商店	*jì niàn pǐn shāng diàn*
supermarket	超级市场	*chāo jí shì chǎng*
toy store	玩具商店	*wán jù shāng diàn*

Friendship stores, 友谊商店 **yǒu yì shāng diàn**, originally set up to provide foreigners with luxury items, can still be found throughout China. They often sell quality goods produced for export and offer a nice selection of souvenirs. Some Friendship stores can send purchases abroad.

sk an Assistant

hen do you open/ ose?	几点开门/关门？	jǐ diǎn kāi mén/guān mén
here's the...?	…在哪里？	...zài nǎ li
cashier	收款处	shōu kuǎn chù
escalator	自动扶梯	zì dòng fú tī
elevator [lift]	电梯	diàn tī
fitting room	试衣间	shì yī jiān
store directory	商店目录	shāng diàn mù lù
n you help me?	你能帮我吗？	nǐ néng bāng wǒ ma
n just looking.	我只是看看。	wǒ zhǐ shì kàn kan
n being helped.	已经有人帮我了。	yǐ jīng yǒu rén bāng wǒ le
o you have...?	你有…吗？	nǐ yǒu...ma
an you show e...?	你能让我看看…吗？	nǐ néng ràng wǒ kàn kan... ma
an you ship/wrap ?	你能把它托运/打包吗？	nǐ néng bǎ tā tuō yùn/dǎ bāo ma
ow much?	多少钱？	duō shǎo qián
nat's all.	就这些。	jiù zhè xiē

or Clothes & Accessories, see page 120.

or Souvenirs, see page 124.

YOU MAY HEAR...

您需要帮忙吗？	nín xú yào bāng mángma	Can I help you?
请稍等。	qǐng shāo děng	One moment.
您要什么？	nín yào shén me	What would you like?
还要别的吗？	hái yào bié de ma	Anything else?

113

YOU MAY SEE…

开门	*kāi mén*	open
关门	*guān mén*	closed
午休关门	*wǔ xiu guān mén*	closed for lunch
试衣间	*shì yī jiān*	fitting room
付款处	*fù kuǎn chù*	cashier
只收现金	*zhī shōu xiàn jīn*	cash only
接受信用卡	*jiē shòu xìn yòng kǎ*	credit cards accepted
营业时间	*yíng yè shí jiān*	business hours
出口	*chū kǒu*	exit

Personal Preferences

I'd like something…	我想要…	*wǒ xiǎng yào…*
cheap/expensive	便宜/贵一点的	*pián yi/ guì yì diǎn de*
larger/smaller	大/小一点的	*dà/xiǎo yì diǎn de*
nicer	好一点的	*hǎo yì diǎn de*
from this region	当地生产的	*dāng dì shēng chǎn de*
Around…yuan.	…元左右的。	*…yuán zuǒ yòu de*
Is it real?	这是真的吗?	*zhè shì zhēn de ma*
Can you show me this/that?	你能让我看看这个/那个吗?	*nǐ néng ràng wǒ kàn kan zhèi ge/nèi ge ma*
That's not quite what I want.	那个不是我要的。	*nà ge bù shì wǒ yào de*
No, I don't like it.	不,我不喜欢这个。	*bù wǒ bú xǐ huan zhè ge*
It's too expensive.	太贵了。	*tài guì le*
I have to think about it.	我要想想。	*wǒ yào xiǎng xiǎng*
I'll take it.	我要了。	*wǒ yào le*

aying & Bargaining

ow much?	多少钱？	*duō shǎo qián*
pay...	我要用…付款	*wǒ yào yòng…fù kuǎn*
in cash	现金	*xiàn jīn*
by credit card	信用卡	*xìn yòng kǎ*
by traveler's check	旅行支票	*lǚ xíng zhī piào*
heque]		
n I use this...card?	我可以用…卡吗？	*wǒ kě yǐ yòng…kǎ ma*
ATM	自动取款机	*zì dòng qǔ kuǎn jī*
credit	信用	*xìn yòng*
debit	借记	*jiè jì*
gift	礼品	*lǐ pǐn*
at's too much.	太贵了。	*tài guì le*
give you...	我给你…	*wǒ gěi nǐ…*
ave only...Ren	我只有…元人民币。	*wǒ zhǐ yǒu …*
in Bi.		*yuán rén mín bì*
that your best price?	是最低价吗？	*shì zuì dī jià ma*
n you give me a scount?	能打折吗？	*néng dǎ zhé ma*
ow do I use this achine?	这机器怎么用？	*zhè jī qì zěn me yòng*
receipt, please.	请给我收据。	*qǐng gěi wǒ shōu jù*

or Numbers, see page 160.

In China, the most commonly accepted form of payment is cash.
Major credit cards may be accepted at larger stores in city centers.

YOU MAY HEAR...

你怎么付款？ *nǐ zěn me fù kuǎn*		How are you paying?
你的信用卡被拒绝了。*nǐ de xìn yòng kǎ bèi jù jué le*		Your credit card has bee declined.
请出示你的身份证。*qǐng chū shì nǐ de shēn fèn zhèng*		ID, please.
我们不接受信用卡。*wǒ men bù jiē shòu xìn yòng kǎ*		We don't accept credit cards.
请付现金。*qǐng fù xiàn jīn*		Cash only, please.
你有零钱/小面值纸币吗？ *nǐ yǒu líng qián/xiǎo miàn zhí zhǐ bì ma*		Do you have change/ small bills [notes]?

Making a Complaint

I'd like...	我想… *wǒ xiǎng...*
to exchange this	换一个 *huàn yí gè*
a refund	退款 *tuì kuǎn*
to see the manager	见经理 *jiàn jīng lǐ*

Services

Can you recommend...?	你能推荐…吗？ *nǐ néng tuī jiàn...ma*
a barber	一位理发师 *yí wèi lǐ fà shī*
a dry cleaner	一家干洗店 *yì jiā gān xǐ diàn*
a hairstylist	一位发型师 *yí wèi fà xíng shī*
a laundromat [launderette]	一家洗衣房 *yì jiā xǐ yī fáng*
a nail salon	一家美甲沙龙 *yì jiā měi jiǎ shā lóng*
a spa	一家温泉 *yì jiā wēn quán*
a travel agency	一家旅行社 *yì jiā lǚ xíng shè*

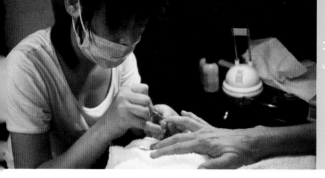

n you…this?	你能…这个吗？ *nǐ néng…zhè ge ma*
alter	改 *gǎi*
clean	洗 *xǐ*
fix [mend]	修 *xiū*
press	熨 *yùn*
hen will it be ready?	什么时候做完？ *shén me shí hòu zuò wán*

air & Beauty

like…	我想… *wǒ xiǎng…*
an appointment	约一个今天/明天的时间 *yuē yí gè jīn*
for today/tomorrow	*tiān/míng tiān de shí jiān*
some color/ highlights	染发/挑染 *rǎn fà/tiāo rǎn*
my hair styled/ blow dried	做/吹头发 *zuò/chuī tóu fà*
a haircut	理发 *lǐ fà*
a trim	剪发 *jiǎn fà*
ot too short.	不要太短。 *bú yào tài duǎn*
horter here.	这里再短一点。 *zhè lǐ zài duǎn yì diǎn*
like…	我想… *wǒ xiǎng…*
a facial	做面部美容 *zuò miàn bù měi róng*

a manicure/ pedicure	修手指甲/脚趾甲	*xiū shǒu zhǐ jia/jiǎo zhǐ jia*
a (sports) massage	要（体育）按摩	*yào (tǐ yù) àn mó*
Do you have/do...?	你提供/做⋯吗？	*nǐ tí gōng/zuò...ma*
acupuncture	针灸	*zhēn jiǔ*
aromatherapy	芳香疗法	*fāng xiāng liáo fǎ*
oxygen treatment	氧气治疗	*yǎng qì zhì liáo*
a sauna	桑拿	*sāng ná*

A number of luxury hotels in China offer facial and body treatments and massage. Some even have unique amenities for spa guests, such as tea centers, taichi (太极 **tài jí**) and yoga lessons. Check with your hotel concierge or a travel agency for a list of spas, their services and prices.

Antiques

How old is it?	有多长历史了？	*yǒu duō cháng lì shǐ le*
Do you have anything from the...period?	你有⋯时期的东西吗？	*nǐ yǒu...shí qī de dōng xi ma*
Do I have to fill out any forms?	我要填表格吗？	*wǒ yào tián biǎo gé ma*
Is there a certificate of authenticity?	有真品证明吗？	*yǒu zhēn pǐn zhèng míng ma*

Clothing

I'd like...	我想要⋯	*wǒ xiǎng yào...*
Can I try this on?	我能试穿吗？	*wǒ néng shì chuān ma*
It doesn't fit.	不合适。	*bù hé shì*

's too...	太···	tài...
big/small	大/小	dà/xiǎo
short/long	短/长	duǎn/cháng
tight/loose	紧/宽	jǐn/kuān
o you have this in ze...?	这款衣服有···号的吗？	zhè kuǎn yī fu yǒu... hào de ma
o you have this in bigger/smaller ze?	这件衣服有大/小一点的吗？	zhè jiàn yī fu yǒu dà/xiǎo yì diǎn de ma

or Numbers, see page 160.

YOU MAY HEAR...

那件衣服很适合你。 *nà jiàn yī fu hěn shì hé nǐ*	That looks great on you.
适合我吗？ *shì hé wǒ ma*	How does it fit?
我们没有你的尺寸 *wǒ men méi yǒu nǐ de chǐ cùn*	We don't have your size.

Western and traditional Chinese clothing is sold at Friendship stores, street markets and local department stores, usually at very reasonable prices. Designer clothing is available at high end boutiques which can be found in larger cities. China is known for its silk production, and silk clothing and fabric (by the yard) can be purchased in many stores.

YOU MAY SEE...

男士的	*nán shì de*	men's
女士的	*nǚ shì de*	women's
儿童的	*ér tóng de*	children's

Colors

I'd like something...	我想要···	*wǒ xiǎng yào...*
beige	米黄	*mǐ huáng*
black	黑色	*hēi sè*
blue	蓝色	*lán sè*
brown	褐色	*hè sè*
green	绿色	*lǜ sè*
gray	灰色	*huī sè*
orange	橙色	*chéng sè*
pink	粉红色	*fěn hóng sè*
purple	紫色	*zǐ sè*
red	红色	*hóng sè*
white	白色	*bái sè*
yellow	黄色	*huáng sè*

Clothes & Accessories

backpack	背包	*bēi bāo*
belt	皮带	*pí dài*
bikini	比基尼	*bǐ jī ní*
blouse	女衬衫	*nǚ chèn shān*
bra	胸罩	*xiōng zhào*
briefs [underpants]	内裤	*nèi kù*
panties	内衣物	*nèi yī wù*
coat	外套	*wài tào*
dress	连衣裙	*lián yī qún*

hat	帽子	*mào zi*
jacket	夹克	*jiá kè*
jeans	牛仔裤	*niú zǎi kù*
pajamas	睡衣	*shuì yī*
pants [trousers]	长裤	*cháng kù*
pantyhose [tights]	裤袜	*kù wà*
purse [handbag]	女式手提包	*nǚ shì shǒu tí bāo*
raincoat	雨衣	*yǔ yī*
scarf	围巾	*wéi jīn*
shirt	衬衫	*chèn shān*
shorts	短裤	*duǎn kù*
skirt	裙子	*qún zi*
socks	袜子	*wà zi*
suit	套服	*tào fú*
sunglasses	太阳镜	*tài yáng jìng*
sweater	毛衣	*máo yī*
sweatshirt	棉毛衫	*mián máoshān*
swimsuit	游泳衣	*yóu yǒng yī*
T-shirt	T恤衫	*tī xù shān*
tie	领带	*lǐng dài*
underwear	内衣	*nèi yī*

Fabric

I'd like…	我想要··· 的 *wǒ xiǎng yào…de*
cotton	棉布 *mián bù*
denim	粗棉布 *cū mián bù*
lace	花边 *huā biān*
leather	皮革 *pí gé*
linen	亚麻布 *yà má bù*
silk	丝绸 *sī chóu*
wool	羊毛 *yáng máo*
Is it machine washable?	可以机洗吗？ *kě yǐ jī xǐ ma*

Shoes

I'd like…	我想要··· *wǒ xiǎng yào…*
high heels/flats	高跟鞋／平跟鞋 *gāo gēn xié/píng gēn xié*
boots	靴子 *xuē zi*
loafers	平底便鞋 *píng dǐ biàn xié*
sandals	凉鞋 *liáng xié*
shoes	鞋子 *xié zi*
slippers	拖鞋 *tuō xié*
sneakers	运动鞋 *yùn dòng xié*
In size…	···号 *…hào*

For Numbers, see page 160.

Sizes

chest measurement	胸围 *xiōng wéi*
waist measurement	腰围 *yāo wéi*
height	身长 *shēn cháng*
petite	小码 *xiǎo mǎ*
extra small (XS)	特小号 *tè xiǎo hào*
small (S)	小号 *xiǎo hào*

edium (M)	中号	*zhōng hào*
rge (L)	大号	*dà hào*
xtra large (XL)	特大号	*tè dà hào*
us size	加大号	*jiā dà hào*

In Friendship stores and places where clothes are made for export, sizes will be given as small, medium and large. Most other clothing stores feature Chinese measurements that combine height and chest size; these measurements appear in centimeters. For example, if you are 170 cm tall (5'6") with a chest measurement of 90 cm (36"), look for clothing marked 170/90. Children's sizes are given by height, in centimeters.

Newsagent & Tobacconist

Do you sell English language newspapers?	你卖英文报纸吗？	*nǐ mài yīng wén bào zhǐ ma*
I'd like...	我想买…	*wǒ xiǎng mǎi...*
a cigar	雪茄	*xuě jiā*
a pack/carton of cigarettes	一包/一条香烟	*yì bāo/yì tiáo xiāng yān*
I'd like...	我想买…	*wǒ xiǎng mǎi...*
a lighter	一个打火机	*yí gè dǎ huǒ jī*
a magazine	一本杂志	*yì běn zá zhì*
matches	火柴	*huǒ chái*
a newspaper	一份报纸	*yí fèn bào zhǐ*
a phone card	一张电话卡	*yì zhāng diàn huà kǎ*
a postcard	一张明信片	*yì zhāng míng xìn piàn*

| a road/town map of... | 一张···道路/市区地图 *yì zhāng...dào lù/shì qū dì tú* |
| stamps | 邮票 *yóu piào* |

124

Photography

I'd like a/an...camera.	我想买一个···照相机。 *wǒ xiǎng mǎi yí gè...zhào xiàng jī*
automatic	自动 *zì dòng*
digital	数码 *shù mǎ*
disposable	一次性 *yí cì xìng*
I'd like...	我想··· *wǒ xiǎng...*
a battery	买一节电池 *mǎi yì jié diàn chí*
digital prints	打印数码照片 *dǎ yìn shù mǎ zhào piàn*
a memory card	买存储卡 *mǎi cún chǔ kǎ*
Can I print digital photos here?	我可以在这里打印数码照片吗？ *wǒ kě yǐ zài zhè li dǎ yìn shù mǎ zhào piàn ma*

Souvenirs

book	书 *shū*
box of chocolates	巧克力 *qiǎo kè lì*
calligraphy supplies	书法用品 *shū fǎ yòng pǐn*
Chinese painting	中国画 *zhōng guó huà*

chopsticks	筷子	*kuài zi*
cloisonné (artwork)	景泰蓝	*jǐng tài lán*
doll	玩具娃娃	*wán jù wá wá*
jade	翡翠	*fěi cuì*
key ring	钥匙圈	*yào shi quān*
lacquerware	漆器	*qī qì*
porcelain	瓷器	*cí qì*
postcard	明信片	*míng xìn piàn*
pottery	陶器	*táo qì*
silk	丝绸	*sī chóu*
T-shirt	T恤衫	*tī xù shān*
toy	玩具	*wán jù*

Can I see this/that? 我能看看这个/那个吗？ *wǒ néng kàn kan zhèi ge/nèi ge ma*

It's in the window/ 在橱窗/陈列橱里。 *zài chú chuāng/*
display case. *chén liè chú lǐ*

I'd like… 我想要… *wǒ xiǎng yào…*

a battery	一节电池	*yì jié diàn chí*
a bracelet	一付手镯	*yí fù shǒu zhuó*
a brooch	一个别针	*yì ge bié zhēn*
a clock	一个钟	*yí ge zhōng*
earrings	一对耳环	*yí duì ěr huán*
a necklace	一条项链	*yì tiáo xiàng liàn*
a ring	一个戒指	*yí ge jiè zhi*
a watch	一块手表	*yí kuài shǒu biǎo*

I'd like… 我想要…的… *wǒ xiǎng yào…de*

copper	铜	*tóng*
crystal	水晶	*shuǐ jīng*
diamonds	钻石	*zuàn shí*
white/yellow gold	白/黄金	*bái/huáng jīn*

pearls	珍珠 *zhēn zhū*
platinum	铂金 *bó jīn*
sterling silver	纯银 *chún yín*

| Is this real? | 这是真的吗？ *zhè shì zhēn de ma* |
| Can you engrave it? | 你能在上面刻字吗？ *nǐ néng zài shàng miàn kè zì ma* |

Typical Chinese souvenirs include silk fabric and clothing, jade and porcelain. Calligraphy supplies, kites, paper cuts and chopsticks are also popular mementos. Souvenirs can be found in malls, department stores and local street markets.
If you're antiquing, note that items dated earlier than 1795 may not be legally exported; any antique leaving China must be affixed with a small red seal, provided by the Cultural Relics Bureau.

Both fine and fashion jewelry can be found throughout China. Most popular items include jade and pearls. Jade is traditionally worn for good luck, as a protection against illness and as an amulet for travelers. Pearls are also part of Chinese tradition; they have been worn by emperors and other nobility. You will also find jewelry made of lacquer and cloisonné, which is a traditional Chinese art. To avoid purchasing imitations, buy from established jewelry shops.

Sport & Leisure

ESSENTIAL

When's the game?	什么时候比赛？ *shén me shí hòu bǐ sài*
Where's the…?	…在哪里？ *…zài nǎ li*
beach	海滩 *hǎi tān*
park	公园 *gōng yuán*
pool	游泳池 *yóu yǒng chí*
Is it safe to swim here?	在这里游泳安全吗？ *zài zhè lǐ yóu yǒng ān quán ma*
Can I rent [hire] golf clubs?	可以租球棒吗？ *kě yǐ zū qiú bàng ma*
How much per hour?	每小时多少钱？ *měi xiǎo shí duō shǎo qián*
How far is it to…?	去…有多远？ *qù…yǒu duō yuǎn*
Show me on the map, please.	请在地图上指给我看。 *qǐng zài dì tú shàng zhǐ gěi wǒ kàn*

Watching Sport

When's the... game/match?	…比赛是什么时候？ *…bǐ sài shì shén me shí hòu*
baseball	棒球 *bàng qiú*
basketball	篮球 *lán qiú*
golf	高尔夫球 *gāo ěr fū qiú*
badminton	羽毛球 *yǔ máo qiú*
ping pong	乒乓球 *pīng pāng qiú*
martial arts	武术 *wǔ shù*
soccer [football]	足球 *zú qiú*
tennis	网球 *wǎng qiú*
volleyball	排球 *pái qiú*
wrestling	摔跤 *shuāi jiāo*

Who's playing?	谁在打球？ *shéi zài dǎ qiú*
Where's the racetrack/stadium?	跑马场/体育场在哪里？ *pǎo mǎ chǎng/tǐ yù chǎng zài nǎ li*
Where can I place a bet?	我可以在哪里下注？ *wǒ kě yǐ zài nǎ li xià Zh*

For Numbers, see page 160.

Early risers will no doubt encounter people practicing taichi (太极 **tài jí**), a combination of martial arts and relaxation movements, in parks throughout China. Some also practice qigong (气功 **qì gōng**), breathing and movement exercises. If you are interested in joining, the crowd would welcome you!
Other sports enjoyed in China include badminton and ping pong. Volleyball courts and swimming pools can be found throughout China. If you're looking for brain exercise instead of a body stretch, try mahjong (麻将 **má jiàng**), a popular Chinese strategy game. Chinese chess and cards are common as well.

aying Sport

here is/are…?	…在哪里？	…zài nǎ li
the golf course	高尔夫球场	gāo ěr fū qiú chǎng
the gym	健身房	jiàn shēn fáng
the park	公园	gōng yuán
the tennis courts	网球场	wǎng qiú chǎng
w much per…?	每…多少钱？	měi…duō shǎo qián
day	天	tiān
hour	小时	xiǎo shí
game	场比赛	chǎng bǐ sài
round	轮比赛	lún bǐ sài
n I rent [hire]…?	我可以租… 吗？	wǒ kě yǐ zū…ma
clubs	球棒	qiú bàng
equipment	设备	shè bèi
a racket	一副球拍	yí fù qiú pāi

the Beach/Pool

here's the beach/ ol?	海滩/游泳池在哪里？	hǎi tān/yóu yǒng chí zài nǎ li
there a…?	有没有…？	yǒu mei yǒu…
kiddie pool	儿童游泳池	ér tong yóu yǒng chí
indoor/outdoor pool	室内/室外游泳池	shì nèi/shì wài yóu yǒng chí
lifeguard	救生员	jiù shēng yuán
it safe…?	…安全吗？	…ān quán ma
to swim	游泳	yóu yǒng
to dive	潜水	qián shuǐ
for children	儿童用	ér tóng yòng

I'd like to rent [hire]...	我想租… *wǒ xiǎng zū...*
a deck chair	一张折叠躺椅 *yì zhāng zhé dié tǎng yǐ*
diving equipment	一套潜水用具 *yí tào qián shuǐ yòng jù*
a jet ski	一套喷气式滑水板 *yí tào pēn qì shì huá shuǐ bǎn*
a motorboat	一艘汽艇 *yì sōu qì tǐng*
a rowboat	一艘划艇 *yì sōu huá tǐng*
snorkeling equipment	潜水设备 *qián shuǐ shè bè*
a surfboard	一块冲浪板 *yí kuài chōng làng bǎn*
a towel	一条毛巾 *yí tiáo máo jīn*
an umbrella	一把伞 *yì bǎ sǎn*
water skis	滑水橇 *huá shuǐ qiāo*
a windsurfer	一只帆船 *yì zhī fān chuán*
For…hours.	共…小时 *gòng...xiǎo shí*

Public beaches can be found along China's east coast. The most popular beaches are often very crowded, so arrive early for a good spot. Beach wear is fairly conservative along China's coast; bathing suits and longer swim shorts are more appropriate than bikinis and short trunks.

Winter Sports

A lift pass for a day/five days, please.	请给我一天/五天的缆车票。 *qǐng gěi wǒ yì tiān/wǔ tiān de lǎn chē piào*
I'd like to rent [hire]...	我想租… *wǒ xiǎng zū...*

boots	一双靴子 *yì shuāng xuē zi*
a helmet	一个头盔 *yí ge tóu kuī*
poles	一对滑雪杖 *yí duì huá xuě zhàng*
skis	一对滑雪板 *yí duì huá xuě bǎn*
a snowboard	一个滑雪单板 *yí ge huá xuě dān bǎn*
snowshoes	一双滑雪靴 *yì shuāng huá xuě xuē*
ese are too g/small.	太大/小。*tài dà/xiǎo*
e there lessons?	可以上课吗？*kě yǐ shàng kè ma*
a beginner.	我是新手。*wǒ shì xīn shǒu*
experienced.	我比较有经验。*wǒ bǐ jiào yǒu jīng yàn*
rail [piste] map, ease.	请给我滑雪路线图。*qǐng gěi wǒ huá xuě lù xiàn tú*

Beijing's lakes freeze during the winter and people often go ice skating. Downhill and cross sountry skiing is popular in northeast China, as are snowboarding and other outdoor winter sports.

YOU MAY SEE...

阻力缆车 *zǔ lì lǎn chē*	drag lift
缆车 *lǎn chē*	cable car
升降椅 *shēng jiàng yǐ*	chair lift
新手 *xīn shǒu*	novice
有一点经验 *yǒu yì diǎn jīng yàn*	intermediate
老手 *lǎo shǒu*	expert
滑雪路线关闭了 *huá xuě lù xiàn guān bì le*	trail [piste] closed

Out in the Country

A map of…, please.	请给我一份···地图。	qǐng gěi wǒ yí fèn… dì tú
this region	这个地区的	zhè ge dì qū de
the walking routes	步行路线	bù xíng lù xiàn
the bike routes	自行车路线	zì xíng chē lù xiàn
the trails	小道	xiǎo dào
Is it…?	这个···吗？	zhè ge …ma
easy	容易	róng yì
difficult	难	nán
far	远	yuǎn
steep	陡峭	dōu qiào
How far is it to…?	离···有多远？	lí…yǒu duō yuǎn
Show me on the map, please.	请在地图上指给我看。	qǐng zài dì tú shàng zhǐ gěi wǒ kàn
I'm lost.	我迷路了。	wǒ mí lù le
Where's the…?	···在哪里？	…zài nǎ li
bridge	桥	qiáo
cave	洞	dòng
cliff	峭壁	qiào bì
desert	沙漠	shā mò
farm	农场	nóng chǎng
field	农田	nóng tián
forest	森林	sēn lín
hill	小山	xiǎo shān
lake	湖	hú
mountain	山	shān
nature preserve	自然保护区	zì rán bǎo hù qū
overlook [viewpoint]	俯视观景点	fǔ shì guān jǐng diǎn
park	公园	gōng yuán
path	道路	dào lù

peak	山顶 *shān dǐng*
picnic area	野餐区 *yě cān qū*
pond	池塘 *chí táng*
river	河流 *hé liú*
sea	大海 *dà hǎi*
(thermal) spring	（热）温泉 *(rè) wēn quán*
stream	小河 *xiǎo hé*
valley	山谷 *shān gǔ*
vineyard	葡萄园 *pú táo yuán*
waterfall	瀑布 *pù bù*

oing Out

SSENTIAL

hat's there to do night?	晚上可以做什么呢？ *wǎn shang kě yǐ zuò shén me ne*
o you have a ogram of events?	你有节目表吗？ *nǐ yǒu jié mù biǎo ma*
hat's playing night?	今晚演什么？ *jīn wǎn yǎn shén me*
here's the...?	…在哪里？ *...zài nǎ lǐ*
downtown area	市中心 *shì zhōng xīn*
bar	酒吧 *jiǔ bā*
dance club	舞蹈俱乐部 *wǔ dǎo jù lè bù*
there a cover arge?	有没有附加费？ *yǒu mei yǒu fù jiā fèi*

Entertainment

Can you recommend...?	你能推荐…吗？	nǐ néng tuī jiàn
a concert	一个音乐会	yí gè yīn yuè huì
a movie	一部电影	yíbù diàn yǐng
an opera	一部歌剧	yí bù gē jù
a play	一部戏剧	yí bù xì jù
When does it start/end?	几点开始/结束？	jǐ diǎn kāi shǐ/jié shù
Where's the...?	…在哪里？	…zài nǎ li
concert hall	音乐厅	yīn yuè tīng
opera house	歌剧院	gē jù yuàn
theater	剧院	jù yuàn
arcade	商场	shāng chǎng
What's the dress code?	有着装要求吗？	yǒu zhuó zhuāng yāo qiú ma
I like...	我喜欢…	wǒ xǐ huan...
classical music	古典音乐	gǔ diǎn yīn yuè
folk music	民族音乐	mín zú yīn yuè
jazz	爵士乐	jué shì yuè
pop music	流行音乐	liú xíng yīn yuè
rap	说唱	shuō chàng

For Tickets, see page 21.

Nightlife is more common in south China than elsewhere; restaurants, bars and cafes usually stay open until at least midnight in the south. *China Daily* and other English language newspapers often list cultural ongoings in major cities. Ask about local events at your hotel or check for events listings in a local newspaper.

YOU MAY HEAR...

请关掉手机。 *qǐng guān diào shǒu jī*

Turn off your cell [mobile] phones, please.

ightlife

hat's there to do night?	晚上可以做什么？	*wǎn shang kě yǐ zuò shén me*
an you commend...?	你能推荐…吗？	*nǐ néng tuī jiàn... ma*
a bar	一个酒吧	*yí ge jiǔ bā*
a casino	一个赌场	*yí ge dǔ chǎng*
a dance club	舞蹈俱乐部	*wǔ dǎo jù lè bù*
a jazz club	爵士乐俱乐部	*jué shì yuè jù lè bù*
a club with hinese music	一家有中国音乐的俱乐部	*yì jiā yǒu zhōng guó yīn yuè de jù lè bù*
there live music?	有没有现场音乐？	*yǒu mei yǒu xiàn chǎng yīn yuè*
ow do I get there?	我怎么去那里	*wǒ zěn me qù nà li*
there a cover narge?	有没有附加费？	*yǒu mei yǒu fù jiā fèi*
et's go dancing.	我们去跳舞吧。	*wǒ men qù tiào wǔ ba*
this area safe t night?	这个地区晚上安全吗？	*zhè ge dì qū wǎn shang ān quán ma*

Special Requirements

Business Travel
Traveling with Children
Disabled Travelers

usiness Travel

SSENTIAL

n here on siness.	我在这里出差。	*wǒ zài zhè li chū chāi*
ere's my business rd.	这是我的名片。	*zhè shì wǒ de míng piàn*
n I have your rd?	可以给我你的名片吗？	*kě yǐ gěi wǒ nǐ de míng piàn ma*
ave a meeting th…	我和…有一个会。	*wǒ hě…yǒu yí gè huì*
here's the…?	…在哪里？	*…zài nǎ li*
business center	商业中心	*shāng yè zhōng xīn*
convention hall	会议厅	*huì yì tīng*
meeting room	会议室	*huì yì shì*

Conducting business in China should be done respectfully. When presenting or receiving a business card in China, be sure to hold the card in both hands. If you have just received a card, do not put it away before reading the card.

Note that Chinese surnames precede given names; therefore, Li Yang should be referred to as Mr Li. Some Chinese professionals have adopted Western first names and name order, though.

On Business

I'm here for a seminar/conference.	我在这儿参加研讨会/讨论会 *wǒ zài zhèr cān jiā yán tǎo huì/tǎo lùn huì*
My name is…	我叫… *wǒ jiào…*
May I introduce my colleague…	我来介绍一下同事… *wǒ lái jiè shào yí xià tóng shì…*
I have a meeting/an appointment with…	我和…有一个会见/预约。 *wǒ hé…yǒu yí gè huì jiàn/yù yuē*
I'm sorry I'm late.	很抱歉我迟到了。 *hěn bào qiàn wǒ chí dào le*
I need an interpreter.	我需要翻译。 *wǒ xū yào fān yì*
You can reach me at the…Hotel.	你可以在…旅馆找到我。 *nǐ kě yǐ zài…lǚ guǎn zhǎo dào wǒ*
I'm here until…	我要在这里呆到… *wǒ yào zài zhè lǐ dāi dào…*

YOU MAY HEAR…

您有预约吗？ *nín yǒu yù yuē ma*	Do you have an appointment?
和谁？ *hé shéi*	With whom?
他 *m* / 她 *f* 在开会。 *tā/tā zài kāi huì*	He/She is in a meeting.
请稍等。 *qǐng shāo děng*	One moment, please.
请坐。 *qǐng zuò*	Have a seat.
您要不要喝点什么？ *nín yào bú yào hē diǎn shén me*	Would you like somethir to drink?
谢谢光临。 *xiè xie guāng lín*	Thank you for coming.

eed to...	我需要··· *wǒ xū yào...*
make a call	打电话 *dǎ diàn huà*
make a photocopy	复印 *fù yìn*
send an e mail	发电子邮件 *fā diàn zǐ yóu jiàn*
send a fax	发传真 *fā chuán zhēn*
send a package (overnight)	寄一个（第二天送达的）包裹 *jì yí gè (dì èr tiān) sòng dá de bāo guǒ*
was a pleasure to eet you.	见到你很高兴。 *jiàn dào nǐ hěn gāo xìng*

r Communications, see page 51.

raveling with Children

SSENTIAL

there a discount r kids?	有儿童折扣吗？ *yǒu ér tóng zhé kòu ma*
an you recommend babysitter?	你能推荐一位保姆吗？ *nǐ néng tuī jiàn yí wèi bǎo mǔ ma*
o you have a child's eat/highchair?	你有儿童座椅/高脚椅吗？ *nǐ yǒu ér tóng zuò yǐ/gāo jiǎo yǐ ma*
Where can I change e baby?	我可以在哪里给孩子换尿布？ *wǒ kě yǐ zài nǎ lǐ gěi hái zi huàn niào bù*

ut & About

an you recommend omething for kids?	你能推荐孩子玩的活动吗？ *nǐ néng tuī jiàn hái zi wán de huó dòng ma*
Where's the...?	···在哪里？ *...zài nǎ lǐ*
amusement park	游乐园 *yóu lè yuán*

arcade	拱廊儿童游戏场 *gǒng láng ér tong yóu xì chǎng*
kiddie [paddling] pool	儿童游泳池 *ér tóng yóu yǒng chí*
park	公园 *gōng yuán*
playground	操场 *cāo chǎng*
zoo	动物园 *dòng wù yuán*
Are kids allowed?	孩子可以进去吗？*hái zi kě yǐ jìn qù ma*
Is it safe for kids?	孩子玩安全吗？*hái zi wán ān quán ma*
Is it suitable for… year olds?	那适合…岁的孩子吗？*nà shì hé…suì de hái zi ma*

For Numbers, see page 160.

YOU MAY HEAR…

真可爱! *zhēn kě ài* — How cute!

他 *m*／她 *f* 叫什么？ *tā/tā jiào shén me* — What's his/her name?

他 *m*／她 *f* 多大了？ *tā/tā duō dà* — How old is he/she?

Baby Essentials

Do you have…?	你有…吗？ *nǐ yǒu…ma*
a baby bottle	奶瓶 *nǎi píng*
baby food	婴儿食品 *yīng ér shí pǐn*
baby wipes	婴儿纸巾 *yīng ér zhǐ jīn*
a car seat	汽车安全座椅 *qì chē ān quán zuò yǐ*
a children's menu/ portion	儿童菜单／份额 *ér tóng cài dān/fèn é*

a child's seat/	儿童座椅/高脚椅 *ér tóng zuò yǐ/gāo jiǎo yǐ*
highchair	
a crib/cot	摇篮/轻便小床 *yáo lán/qīng biàn xiǎo chuáng*
diapers [nappies]	尿不湿 *niào bù shī*
formula [baby food]	婴儿奶粉 *yīng ér nǎi fěn*
a pacifier [soother]	奶嘴 *nǎizuǐ*
a playpen	游戏围栏 *yóu xì wéi lán*
a stroller	婴儿车 *yīng ér chē*
[pushchair]	
n I breastfeed	我可以在这里喂孩子吃母奶吗？ *wǒ kě yǐ*
e baby here?	*zài zhè li wèi hái zi chī mǔ nǎi ma*
here can I	我可以在哪里喂孩子吃母奶/给孩子换
eastfeed/change	尿布？ *wǒ kě yǐ zài nǎ li wèi hái zi chī mǔ nǎi/*
e baby?	*gěi hái zi huàn niào bù*

r Dining with Children, see page 68.

abysitting

n you recommend	你能推荐一位保姆吗？ *nǐ néng tuī jiàn yī*
babysitter?	*wèi bǎo mǔ ma*
hat do you/they	你们/他们收费是多少？ *nǐ men/tā men*
arge?	*shōu fèi shì duō shǎo*

I'll be back by...	我在···之前回来。	*wǒ zài...zhī qián huí lái*
I can be reached at...	打···可以找到我。	*dǎ...kě yǐ zhǎo dào wǒ*

For Time, see page 163.

Health & Emergency

Can you recommend a pediatrician?	你能推荐一位儿科医生吗？	*nǐ néng tuī jiàn yí wèi ér kē yī shēng ma*
My child is allergic to...	我的孩子对···过敏。	*wǒ de hái zi duì... guò mǐn*
My child is missing.	我的孩子不见了。	*wǒ de hái zi bù jiàn le*
Have you seen a boy/girl?	你看到一个男孩/女孩吗？	*nǐ kàn dào yí ge nán hái/nǚ hái ma*

For Meals & Cooking, see page 70.

For Health, see page 148.

For Police, see page 146.

Disabled Travelers

ESSENTIAL

Is there...?	有···吗？	*yǒu...ma*
access for the disabled	残疾人通道	*cán jí rén tōng dào*
a wheelchair ramp	轮椅坡道	*lún yǐ pō dào*
a disabled accessible toilet	一间残疾人可用的洗手间	*yì jiān cán jí rén kě yòng de xǐ shǒu jiān*
I need...	我需要···	*wǒ xū yào...*
assistance	帮助	*bāng zhù*
an elevator [a lift]	电梯	*diàn tī*
a ground floor room	一个一楼的房间	*yí gè yī lóu de fáng jiān*

king for Assistance

I …	我…	wǒ…
disabled	是残疾人	shì cán jí rén
visually impaired	视力不好	shì lì bù hǎo
hearing impaired/deaf	听力不好/耳聋	tīng lì bù hǎo/ěr lóng
unable to walk far/ use the stairs	不能走远路/走台阶	bù néng zǒu yuǎn lù/zǒu tái jiē
ease speak louder.	请大声讲话。	qǐng dà shēng jiǎng huà
n I bring my heelchair?	我可以带轮椅吗？	wǒ kě yǐ dài lún yǐ ma
e guide dogs rmitted?	允许导盲犬吗？	yǔn xǔ dǎo máng quǎn ma
n you help me?	你可以帮我吗？	nǐ kě yǐ bāng wǒ ma
ease open/hold e door.	请打开/拉着门。	qǐng dǎ kāi/lā zhe mén

In an Emergency

SENTIAL

lp!	救命！	*jiù mìng*
away!	走开！	*zǒu kāi*
p, thief!	站住，抓贼！	*zhàn zhù zhuā zéi*
t a doctor!	找位医生！	*zhǎo wèi yī shēng*
e!	着火啦！	*zháo huǒ lā*
lost.	我迷路了。	*wǒ mí lù le*
n you help me?	你可以帮我吗？	*nǐ kě yǐ bāng wǒ ma*

he emergency numbers in China are as follows: **110**, police; **20**, ambulance; **119**, fire emergency. For the telephone directory, ial **114**. Numbers for local emergency services should be available at our hotel or the tourist information office.

OU MAY HEAR...

填好这份表格。 *tián hǎo zhè fèn biǎo gé*	Fill out this form.
请出示你的身份证。 *qǐng chū hì nǐ de shēn fèn zhèng*	Your identification, please.
是什么时候/在哪里发生的？ hì shén me shí hou/zài nǎ li fā shēng de	When/Where did it happen?
他 *m*/她 *f* 长得什么样？ ā/tā zhǎng de shén me yàng	What does he/she look like?

Police

ESSENTIAL

Call the police!	给警察打电话！	*gěi jǐng chá dǎ diàn huà*
Where's the police station?	警察局在哪里？	*jǐng chá jú zài nǎ li*
There was an accident/an attack.	出事故/有人受攻击了。	*chū shì gù/yǒu rén shòu gōng jǐ le*
My child is missing.	我的孩子不见了。	*wǒ de hái zi bù jiàn le*
I need...	我需要···	*wǒ xū yào...*
an interpreter	一个翻译	*yí gè fān yì*
to contact my lawyer	和我的律师联系	*hé wǒ de lǜ shī lián xì*
to make a phone call	打电话	*dǎ diàn huà*
I'm innocent.	我是无辜的。	*wǒ shì wú gū de*

...ime & Lost Property

...ant to report...	我想报告一次…事件。	*wǒ xiǎng bào gào yí cì…shì jiàn*
a mugging	抢劫	*qiǎng jié*
a rape	强奸	*qiáng jiān*
a theft	偷窃	*tōu qiè*
...as mugged/...obed.	我被抢/遭抢劫了。	*wǒ bèi qiǎng/zāo qiǎng jié le*
...st my...	我的…丢了。	*wǒ de…diū le*
...v...was stolen.	我的…被偷了。	*wǒ…de bèi tōu le*
backpack	背包	*bēi bāo*
bicycle	自行车	*zì xíng chē*
camera	照相机	*zhào xiàng jī*
(rental [hire]) car	（租的）汽车	*(zū de) qì chē*
computer	计算机	*jì suàn jī*
credit card	信用卡	*xìn yòng kǎ*
jewelry	首饰	*shǒu shì*
money	钱	*qián*
passport	护照	*hù zhào*
purse [handbag]	提包	*tí bāo*
traveler's checks [cheques]	旅行支票	*lǚ xíng zhī piào*
wallet	钱包	*qián bāo*
...eed a police report.	我要报警。	*wǒ yào bào jǐng*
...here is the British/...merican/Irish ...mbassy?	英国/美国/爱尔兰大使馆在哪里？	*yīng guó/měi guó/ài ěr lán dà shǐ guǎn zài nǎ li*
...eed an interpreter.	我需要一位口译员。	*wǒ xū yào yī wèi Kǒu yì yuán*

147

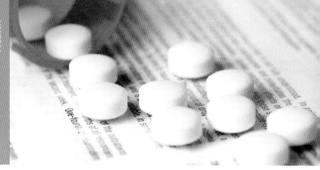

Health

ESSENTIAL

I'm sick.	我病了。	*wǒ bìng le*
I need an English speaking doctor.	我需要说英语的医生。	*wǒ xū yào shuō yīng yǔ de yī shēng*
It hurts here.	这里疼。	*zhè lǐ téng*
I have a stomachache.	我肚子疼。	*wǒ dù zi téng*

Finding a Doctor

Can you recommend a doctor/dentist?	你能推荐一位医生/牙医吗？	*nǐ néng tuī jiàn yí wèi yī shēng/yá yī ma*
Can the doctor come here?	医生能来这里吗？	*yī shēng néng lái zhè li ma*
I need an English speaking doctor.	我需要说英语的医生。	*wǒ xū yào shuō yīng yǔ de yī shēng*
What are the office hours?	办公时间是什么时候？	*bàn gōng shí jiān shì shén me shí hou*

like an	我想要…预约。	wǒ xiǎng yào… yù yuē
...pointment for...		
today	今天	jīn tiān
tomorrow	明天	míng tiān
as soon as possible	尽快	jǐn kuài
urgent.	很急。	hěn jí

...mptoms

......	我…	wǒ...
bleeding	在流血	zài liú xuè
constipated	便秘	biàn bì
dizzy	头晕	tóu yūn
nauseous	恶心	ě xīn
vomiting	呕吐	ǒu tù
...urts here.	这里疼。	zhè li téng
...ave...	我…	wǒ...
an allergic reaction	有过敏反应	yǒu guò mǐn fǎn yìng
chest pain	胸口痛	xiōng kǒu tòng
cramps	有痉挛	yǒu jìng luán
diarrhea	腹泻	fù xiè
an earache	耳朵疼	ěr duo téng
a fever	发烧	fā shāo
pain	身上疼	shēn shàng téng
a rash	出疹子了	chū zhěn zi le
a sprain	有扭伤	yǒu niǔ shāng
some swelling	有浮肿	yǒu fú zhǒng
a sore throat	喉咙痛	hóu lóng tòng
a stomachache	肚子疼	dù zi téng
sunstroke	中暑	zhòng shǔ
...e been sick	我已经病了…天了。	wǒ yǐ jīng bìng le...
...r...days.		tiān le

...r Numbers, see page 160.

Conditions

I'm anemic.	我贫血。 *wǒ pín xuě*
I'm allergic to antibiotics/penicillin.	我对抗生素/青霉素过敏。 *wǒ duì kàng shēng sù/qīng méi sù guò mǐn*
I have…	我有… *wǒ yǒu…*
arthritis	关节炎 *guān jié yán*
asthma	气喘病 *qì chuǎn bìng*
diabetes	糖尿病 *táng niào bìng*
epilepsy	癫痫患者 *diān xián huàn zhě*
a heart condition	心脏病 *xīn zàng bìng*
high/low blood pressure	高/低血压 *gāo/dī xuè yā*
I'm on…	我在吃… *wǒ zài chī…*

For Meals & Cooking, see page 70.

Treatment

Do I need a prescription/medicine?	我需要处方/吃药吗？ *wǒ xū yào chū fāng/chī yào ma*
Can you prescribe a generic drug [unbranded medication]?	你能开常用药吗？ *nǐ néng kāi cháng yòng yào ma*
Where can I get it?	我在哪里可以买到？ *wǒ zài nǎ li kě yǐ mǎi dào*
Is this over the counter?	这是无处方药吗？ *zhè shì wú chū fāng yào ma*

For Pharmacy, see page 153.

YOU MAY HEAR...

怎么了？ zěn me le	What's wrong?
哪里疼？ nǎ li téng	Where does it hurt?
这里疼吗？ zhè li téng ma	Does it hurt here?
你在吃药吗？ nǐ zài chī yào ma	Are you on medication?
你对什么过敏吗？ nǐ duì shén me guò mǐn ma	Are you allergic to anything?
把嘴张开。 bǎ zuǐ zhāng kāi	Open your mouth.
深呼吸。 shēn hū xī	Breathe deeply.
请咳嗽。 qǐng ké sou	Cough please.
去看专家。 qù kàn zhuān jiā	See a specialist.
去医院。 qù yī yuàn	Go to the hospital.
它… tā…	It's…
骨折了 gǔ zhé le	broken
会传染 huì chuán rǎn	contagious
被感染了 bèi gǎn rǎn le	infected
被扭伤了 bèi niǔ shāng le	sprained
不要紧 bú yào jǐn	nothing serious

Hospital

Notify my family, please.	请通知我家人。 qǐng tōng zhī wǒ jiā rén
I'm in pain.	我很疼。 wǒ hěn téng
I need a doctor/nurse.	我需要医生/护士。 wǒ xū yào yī shēng/hù shi
When are visiting hours?	探病时间是什么时候？ tàn bìng shí jiān shì shén me shí hou
I'm visiting…	我来看望… wǒ lái kàn wàng…

Dentist

I have...	我···	*wǒ...*
a broken tooth	有一颗断牙	*yǒu yì kē duàn yá*
lost a filling	的补牙填料掉了	*de bǔ yá tián liào diào le*
a toothache	牙疼	*yá téng*
Can you fix this denture?	你能修这个假牙吗？	*nǐ néng xiū zhè ge jiǎ yá ma*

Gynecologist

I have cramps/ a vaginal infection.	我有经期腹痛/阴道感染。	*wǒ yǒu jīng qī fù tòng/yīn dào gǎn rǎn*
I missed my period.	我月经没来。	*wǒ yuè jīng méi lái*
I'm on the Pill.	我在吃避孕药。	*wǒ zài chī bì yùn yào*
I'm (...months) pregnant.	我怀孕（···月）了。	*wǒ huái yùn (...yuè) le*
I'm not pregnant.	我没怀孕。	*wǒ méi huái yùn*
My last period was...	我上次月经是···	*wǒ shàng cì yuè jīng shì...*

Optician

I lost...	我丢了···	*wǒ diū le...*
a contact lens	隐形眼镜	*yǐn xíng yǎn jìng*
my glasses	我的眼镜	*wǒ de yǎn jìng*
a lens	一个镜片	*yí gè jìng piàn*

Payment & Insurance

How much?	多少钱？	*duō shǎo qián*
Can I pay by credit card?	我可以用信用卡付款吗？	*wǒ kě yǐ yòng xìn yòng kǎ fù kuǎn ma*
I have insurance.	我有保险。	*wǒ yǒu bǎo xiǎn*
I need a receipt for my insurance.	我需要一张给保险的收据。	*wǒ xū yào yì zhāng gěi bǎo xiǎn de shōu jù*

SSENTIAL

here's the armacy [chemist]?	药房在哪里？ *yào fáng zài nǎ li*
hat time does it en/close?	它什么时候开门/关门？ *tā shén me shí hou kāi mén/guān mén*
hat would you commend for...?	你…推荐什么呢？ *nǐ...tuī jiàn shén me ne*
w much do I take?	我要吃多少呢？ *wǒ yào chī duō shǎo ne*
n you fill [make] this prescription?	你能提供这种处方药吗？ *nǐ néng tí gōng zhè zhǒng chǔ fāng yào ma*
n allergic to...	我对…过敏？ *wǒ duì...guò mǐn*

You will find 24 hour pharmacies in larger cities. Standard pharmacy hours are 9:00 a.m. to 9:00 p.m. In the event of an emergency, visit the nearest hospital emergency center. China is well known for its traditional pharmacies, 中药 **zhōng yào**, which provide many natural remedies: dried and preserved plants, seeds, animal parts and minerals. You may also find acupuncture needles and other holistic healing tools at these locations.

/hat to Take

ow much do I take?	我吃多少呢？ *wǒ chī duō shǎo ne*
ow often?	多长时间吃一次？ *duō cháng shí jiān chī yí cì*
it safe for children?	对孩子安全吗？ *duì hái zi ān quán ma*
n taking...	我在吃… *wǒ zài chī...*

Are there side effects?	有副作用吗？	*yǒu fù zuò yòng ma*
I need something for...	我需要治…的药。	*wǒ xū yào zhì…de yào*
a cold	感冒	*gǎn mào*
a cough	咳嗽	*ké sou*
diarrhea	腹泻	*fù xiè*
a hangover	宿醉	*sù zuì*
a headache	头疼	*tóu téng*
insect bites	虫咬	*chóng yǎo*
motion [travel] sickness	晕动病	*yùn dòng bìng*
a sore throat	喉咙痛	*hóu lóng tòng*
sunburn	晒伤	*shài shāng*
a toothache	牙疼	*yá téng*
an upset stomach	肠胃不适	*cháng wèi bú shì*

Basic Suplies

I'd like...	我要…	*wǒ yào...*
acetaminophen [paracetamol]	泰诺	*tài nuò*
aftershave	须后水	*xū hòu shuǐ*
aspirin	阿斯匹林	*ā sī pǐ lín*

bandages	绷带 *bēng dài*
a comb	一把梳子 *yì bǎ shū zi*
condoms	避孕套 *bì yùn tào*
contact lens solution	隐形眼镜清洗液 *yǐn xíng yǎn jìng qīng xǐ yè*
deodorant	止汗露 *zhǐ hàn lù*
a hairbrush	一把梳子 *yì bǎ shū zi*
hairspray	喷发剂 *pēn fà jì*
ibuprofen	布洛芬 *bù luò fēn*
insect repellent	杀虫剂 *shā chóng jì*
lotion	乳液 *rǔ yè*
a nail file	指甲锉刀 *zhǐ jiǎ cuò dāo*
a (disposable) razor	（一次性）剃须刀 *(yí cì xìng) tì xū dāo*
razor blades	刀片 *dāo piàn*
sanitary napkins [pads]	卫生巾 *wèi shēng jīn*
shampoo/ conditioner	香波/护发素 *xiāng bō/hù fà sù*

YOU MAY SEE...

一天一次/三次 *yì tiān yí cì/ sān cì*	once/three times a day
片剂 *piàn jì*	tablet
滴剂 *dī jì*	drop
用茶匙吃 *yòng chá chí chí*	teaspoon
饭后/饭前/吃饭时服用 *fàn hòu/ fàn qián/chī fàn shí fú yòng*	after/before/with meals
空腹服用 *kōng fù fú yòng*	on an empty stomach
整个咽下 *zhěng gè yàn xià*	swallow whole
可能使人困倦 *kě néng shǐ rén kùn juàn*	may cause drowsiness
只能外用 *zhǐ néng wài yòng*	for external use only

soap	肥皂	*féi zào*
sunscreen	防晒霜	*fáng shài shuāng*
tampons	月经栓	*yuè jīng shuān*
tissues	面巾纸	*miàn jīn zhǐ*
toilet paper	卫生纸	*wèi shēng zhǐ*
toothpaste	牙膏	*yá gāo*

For Baby Essentials, see page 140.

The Basics

Grammar

Verbs

Chinese verbs are not conjugated. There is one basic verb form that is used f
every person and time (present, past, future) Actions at different times are
usually expressed using adverbs of time such as yesterday, tomorrow, etc.

He walks to school everyday. (habitual action)
他每天走路去上学.
tā měi tiān zǒu lù qù shàng xié

We want to go to school on foot. (talking about a plan)
我们要走路去上学。
wǒ men yào zǒu lù qù shàng xié

I walked to school. (talking about a past event)
我是走路去学校的。
wǒ shì zǒu lù qù xié xiào de

Time can also be expressed by using the particle 过 (**guò**) and/or 了 (**le**). In
below example, both are used:

I have eaten.　　　　　　我吃过了。 *wǒ chī guò le*

...ouns

...ere are no plural forms for Chinese nouns, with few exceptions. Whether ...e noun is singular or plural is determined from the context or by a number ...odifying the noun.

...y bag is missing.
...的包不见了。
...*de (yí ge) bāo bú jiàn le* (use 'yí ge' or nothing before or after 'bāo')

...y bags are missing.
...的包都不见了。
...*de dōu bú jiàn le* (the word 'dōu' indicate more than one)

...onouns

...rsonal pronouns in Chinese are:

	我	*wǒ*
...u	你	*nǐ*
	他	*tā*
...e	她	*tā*
	它	*tā*
...	我们	*wǒ men*
...u (pl)	你们	*nǐ men*
...ey	他们 **m** / 她们 **f**	*tā men/tā men*

...rsonal pronouns do not require different verb forms:

...m	我是	*wǒ shì*
...e is	他是	*tā shì*
...ey are	他们是	*tā men shì*

... make a pronoun possessive, just add 的 (**de**) after the pronoun:
...y 我的 *wǒ de* (Literally: I + 'de')

Word Order

Word order in Chinese is usually as in English: subject, verb, object. This var[?] though depending on the emphasis of the sentence.

I would like a cup of tea.
我想要杯茶。
wǒ xiǎng yào bēi chá

Yes/No questions are formed by adding the question word 吗 (**ma**) at the end of the statement:

Is this the ticket office? (Literally: This is ticket office?)
这是售票处吗？
zhè shì shòu piào chù ma

Other questions are formed by inserting specific question words — who, what, where, when, how many, in the place in the statement where the information asked for would come:

Where is the ticket office?
售票处在哪里？
shòu piào chù zài nǎ li

The Chinese is literally, 'Ticket office is *where*?' 'Where' follows the verb bec[?] the answer would also follow the verb, 'The ticket office is *here*.'

Negation & Affirmation

不 (**bú**) or 没 (**méi**) is added before the verb to indicate negation. While [?] preceeds the verb to be, 没 is used in front of 有 (**yǒu**) and to negate the action already completed:

I am not on vacation.
我不是在度假。
wǒ bú shì zài dù jià

I have not bought the ticket.
我还没有买票。
wǒ hái méi yǒu mǎi piào.

repeat the verb that was used in the question for affirmations or add 不 (**bù**) before the verb for negations:

Would you like tea?

你想喝茶吗？

nǐ xiǎng hē chá ma

Yes, I would.

想。

xiǎng

No, thank you.

不想。

bù xiǎng

Imperatives

Usually, 吧 (**ba**) or 呀 (**ya**) is added at the end of a statement to express a command politely:

Buy the ticket! 买票吧！ *mǎi piào ba*

Adjectives

Adjectives with two or more syllables in Chinese usually have the character 的 (**de**) at the end and precede the noun they modify:

A good meal 好吃的饭 *hào chī de fàn*

Adverbs

Adverbs in Chinese are usually followed by 地 (**de**) and precede the verbs they modify:

Work carefully 认真地工作 *rèn zhēn de gōng zuò*

Numbers

ESSENTIAL

0	零	líng
1	一	yī
2	二	èr
3	三	sān
4	四	sì
5	五	wǔ
6	六	liù
7	七	qī
8	八	bā
9	九	jiǔ
10	十	shí
11	十一	shí yī
12	十二	shí èr
13	十三	shí sān
14	十四	shí sì
15	十五	shí wǔ
16	十六	shí liù
17	十七	shí qī
18	十八	shí bā
19	十九	shí jiǔ
20	二十	èr shí
21	二十一	èr shí yī
22	二十二	èr shí èr
30	三十	sān shí
31	三十一	sān shí yī
40	四十	sì shí
50	五十	wǔ shí

	六十	*liù shí*
	七十	*qī shí*
	八十	*bā shí*
	九十	*jiǔ shí*
0	一百	*yì bǎi*
1	一百零一	*yì bǎi líng yī*
0	二百	*èr bǎi*
0	五百	*wǔ bǎi*
00	一千	*yì qiān*
,000	一万	*yí wàn*
00,000	一百万	*yì bǎi wàn*

n Chinese, there are general numbers, listed above, used for
alking about sums of money, phone numbers, etc. There is also
a system for combining a number with an object-specific counter.
This system groups objects into types according to shape and size;
there are specific ways to count flat objects, machines, animals, people,
etc. When you're unsure of the correct counter, you can try using the
general numbers above or the all-purpose counters on page 162.

All purpose Counters

1	一个	*yí gè*
2	两个	*liǎng*
3	三个	*sān gè*
4	四个	*sì gè*
5	五个	*wǔ gè*
6	六个	*liù gè*
7	七个	*qī gè*
8	八个	*bā gè*
9	九个	*jiǔ gè*
10	十个	*shí gè*

Note that the counter usually precedes the word it qualifies:

I'd like an apple.

我想要一个苹果。

wǒ xiǎng yào yī gè píng guǒ

I'd like two apples.

我想要两个苹果。

wǒ xiǎng yào liǎng gè píng guǒ

Other Counters

	thin, flat objects	(of any shape)	(of any size)
1	一张 *yī zhāng*	一片 *yí piàn*	一包 *yí bāo*
2	两张 *liǎng zhāng*	两片 *liǎng piàn*	两包 *liǎng*
3	三张 *sān zhāng*	三片 *sān piàn*	三包 *sān bā*
4	四张 *sì zhāng*	四片 *sì piàn*	四包 *sì bāo*
5	五张 *wǔ zhāng*	五片 *wǔ piàn*	五包 *wǔ bā*

dinal Numbers

st	第一	dì yī
ond	第二	dì èr
rd	第三	dì sān
urth	第四	dì sì
h	第五	dì wǔ

easurements of Action

ce	一次	yí cì
ce	两次	liǎng cì
ee times	三次	sān cì

me

SENTIAL

at time is it?	几点了？	jǐ diǎn le
noon [midday].	现在是中午。	xiàn zài shì zhōng wǔ
midnight.	午夜	wǔ yè
m one o'clock to o'clock.	从一点到两点	cóng yì diǎn dào liǎng diǎn
e after [past] three.	三点过五分	sān diǎn guò wǔ fēn
uarter to four.	差一刻四点	chà yí kè sì diǎn
:0 a.m./p.m.	上午/下午五点半	shàng wǔ/xià wǔ wǔ diǎn bàn

Days

ESSENTIAL

Monday	星期一	*xīng qī yī*
Tuesday	星期二	*xīng qī èr*
Wednesday	星期三	*xīng qī sān*
Thursday	星期四	*xīng qī sì*
Friday	星期五	*xīng qī wǔ*
Saturday	星期六	*xīng qī liù*
Sunday	星期天	*xīng qī tiān*

Dates

yesterday	昨天	*zuó tiān*
today	今天	*jīn tiān*
tomorrow	明天	*míng tiān*
day	天	*tiān*
week	星期	*xīng qī*
month	月	*yuè*
year	年	*nián*

In China, dates are written in the following order: year 年 (**nián**), month 月 (**yuè**) and date 日 (**rì**). For example, October 12, 2006 in Chinese would be 2006 年 **10** 月 **12** 日. Note that while months can be represented as on page 165, Arabic numbers are also used.

onths

uary	一月	*yī yuè*
ruary	二月	*èr yuè*
rch	三月	*sān yuè*
il	四月	*sì yuè*
y	五月	*wǔ yuè*
e	六月	*liù yuè*
y	七月	*qī yuè*
gust	八月	*bā yuè*
tember	九月	*jiǔ yuè*
ober	十月	*shí yuè*
vember	十一月	*shí yī yuè*
cember	十二月	*shí èr yuè*

asons

During the…	在…	*zài…*
spring	春天	*chūn tiān*
summer	夏天	*xià tiān*
fall [autumn]	秋天	*qiū tiān*
winter	冬天	*dōng tiān*

lidays

Day of the 1st Lunar Month: Spring Festival (Chinese New Year)

rch 8: International Woman's Day

il 5: Tomb Sweeping Day

y 1: International Labor Day

y 5 (Lunar Calendar): Dragon Boat Festival

e 1: Children's Day

gust 15: (Lunar Calendar) Mid-Autumn Festival (Moon cake Day)

ober 1: National Day

ober 15 (Lunar Calendar): Mid Autumn Festival (Moon cake Day)

Traditional holidays, such as Chinese New Year, or Spring
Festival, follow the lunar calendar and, so, dates vary annually.
Chinese New Year is an important holiday in China, celebrated
with gifts, decorations, traditional food and fireworks. It ends on the
fifteenth day of the lunar new year with the Lantern Festival, which
includes festivities such as a lantern parade and lion dance.

Conversion Tables

When you know	Multiply by	To find
ounces	28.3	grams
pounds	0.45	kilograms
inches	2.54	centimeters
feet	0.3	meters
miles	1.61	kilometers
square inches	6.45	sq. centimeters
square feet	0.09	sq. meters
square miles	2.59	sq. kilometers
pints (U.S./Brit)	0.47/0.56	liters
gallons (U.S./Brit)	3.8/4.5	liters
Fahrenheit	5/9, after 32	Centigrade
Centigrade	9/5, then +32	Fahrenheit

Mileage			
1 km	0.62 miles	20 km	12.4 miles
5 km	3.1 miles	50 km	31 miles
10 km	6.2 miles	100 km	61 miles

Measurement

gram	1 克 kè	= 0.035 oz.
kilogram (kg)	1 公斤 gōng jīn	= 2.2 lb
liter (l)	1 公升 gōng shēng	= 1.06 U.S./ 0.88 Brit. quarts
centimeter (cm)	1 厘米 lí mǐ	= 0.4 inch
meter (m)	1 米 mǐ	= 3.28 feet
kilometer (km)	1 公里 gōng lǐ	= 0.62 mile

Temperature

-40°C – -40°F	-1°C – 30°F	20°C – 68°F
-30°C – -22°F	0°C – 32°F	25°C – 77°F
-20°C – -4°F	5°C – 41°F	30°C – 86°F
-10°C – 14°F	10°C – 50°F	35°C – 95°F
-5°C – 23°F	15°C – 59°F	

Oven Temperature

100°C – 212°F	177°C – 350°F
121°C – 250°F	204°C – 400°F
149°C – 300°F	260°C – 500°F

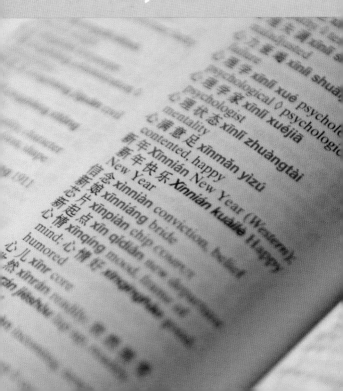

Dictionary

...m. 上午 shàng wǔ
...bey 修道院 xiū dào yuàn
...cept v 接受 jiē shòu
...cess 进入 jìn rù
...cident 事故 shì gù
...commodation 住宿 zhù sù
...count n 账户 zhàng hù
...upuncture 针灸 zhēn jiǔ
...apter 变压器 biàn yā qì
...dress 地址 dì zhǐ
...mission 入场 rù chǎng
...ter 以后 yǐ hòu
...ternoon 下午 xià wǔ
...tershave 须后水 xū hòu shuǐ
...e 年龄 nián líng
...ency 代办处 dài bàn chù
...DS 爱滋病 ài zī bìng
...r conditioning 空调 kōng tiáo
...r pump 气筒 qì tǒng
...rline 航空公司 háng kōng gōng sī
...rmail 航空信 háng kōng xìn
...rplane 飞机 fēi jī
...rport 飞机场 fēi jī chǎng

aisle 过道 guò dào
aisle seat 靠过道的位子 kào guò dào de wèi zi
allergic 过敏 guò mǐn
allergic reaction 过敏反应 guò mǐn fǎn yìng
allow v 允许 yǔn xǔ
alone 单独 dān dú
alter v (clothing) 改 gǎi
alternate route 变更路线 biàn gēng lù xiàn
aluminum foil 厨房锡纸 chú fáng xī zhǐ
amazing 令人惊奇的 lìng rén jīng qí de
ambulance 救护车 jiù hù chē
American 美国人 měi guó rén
amusement park 游乐园 yóu lè yuán
anemic 贫血 pín xuè
anesthesia 麻醉 má zuì
animal 动物 dòng wù
ankle 脚腕 jiǎo wàn
antibiotic 抗生素 kàng shēng sù

| **adj** adjective | **BE** British English | **prep** preposition |
| **adv** adverb | **n** noun | **v** verb |

antiques store 古董店 gǔ dǒng diàn

antiseptic cream 消毒药膏 xiāo dú yào gāo

anything 任何东西 rèn hé dōng xī

apartment 公寓 gōng yù

appendix (body part) 盲肠 máng cháng

appetizer 开胃菜 kāi wèi cài

appointment 约会 yuē huì

arcade 拱廊儿童游戏场 gǒng láng ér tóng yóu xì chǎng

area code 区号 qū hà

arm 胳膊 gē bo

aromatherapy 芳香疗法 fāng xiāng liáo fǎ

around (the corner) 拐角处 guǎi jiǎo chù

arrivals (airport) 抵达 dǐ dá

arrive v 到达 dào dá

artery 动脉 dòng mài

arthritis 关节炎 guān jié yán

Asian (restaurant) 亚洲 yà zhōu

aspirin 阿斯匹林 ā sī pǐ lín

asthmatic 气喘 qì chuǎn

ATM 自动取款机 zì dòng qǔ kuǎn jī

ATM card 自动取款卡 zì dòng qǔ kuǎn kǎ

attack (on person) 攻击 gōng jī

attend v 出席 chū xí

attraction (place) 游览胜地 lǎn shèng dì

attractive 有吸引力的 yǒu xī yǐn lì de

Australian 澳大利亚人 ào dà lì yà rén

automatic 自动 zì dòng

automatic car 自动汽车 zì dòng qì chē

B

baby 婴儿 yīng ér

baby bottle 奶瓶 nǎi píng

baby wipe 婴儿纸巾 yīng ér zhǐ jīn

babysitter 保姆 bǎo mǔ

back (body part) 背部 bèi bù

backpack 背包 bēi bāo

bag 袋子 dài zi

baggage [BE] 行李 xíng li

baggage claim 行李认领 xíng li rèn lǐng

baggage ticket 行李票 xíng li piào

bakery 面包店 miàn bāo diàn

ballet 芭蕾 bā léi

bandage 绷带 bēng dài

bank 银行 yín háng

bar (place) 酒吧 jiǔ bā

barbecue 烤肉 kǎo ròu

rber 理发师 lǐ fà shī

seball 棒球 bàng qiú

sket (grocery store) 购物篮子 gòu wù lán zi

sketball 篮球 lán qiú

throom 浴室 yù shì

ttery 电池 diàn chí

ttleground 战场 zhàn chǎng

v 是 shì

ach 海滩 hǎi tān

autiful 美丽 měi lì

d 床 chuáng

d and breakfast 带早餐的旅店 dài zǎo cān de lǚ diàn

gin v 开始 kāi shǐ

fore 以前 yǐ qián

ginner (skill level) 初学者 chū xué zhě

hind (direction) 后面 hòu mian

ige 米黄色 mǐ huáng sè

lt 皮带 pí dài

rth 铺位 pùwèi

st 最好 zuì hǎo

tter 更好 gèng hǎo

cycle 自行车 zì xíng chē

g 大 dà

gger 更大 gèng dà

ke route 自行车路线 zì xíng chē lù xiàn

ikini 比基尼泳装 bǐ jī ní yǒng zhuāng

bill v (charge) 开付款单 kāi fù kuǎn dān; ~ n (money) 纸币 zhǐ bì; ~ n (of sale) 账单 zhàng dān

bird 鸟 niǎo

birthday 生日 shēng rì

black 黑色 hēi sè

bladder 膀胱 páng guāng

bland 无味 wú wèi

blanket 毯子 tǎn zi

bleed v 流血 liú xuè

blood 血液 xuè yè

blood pressure 血压 xuè yā

blouse 女衬衫 nǚ chèn shān

blue 蓝色 lán sè

board v 登机 dēng jī

boarding pass 登机牌 dēng jī pái

boat 小船 xiǎo chuán

bone 骨头 gǔ tou

book 书 shū

bookstore 书店 shū diàn

boots 靴子 xuē zi

boring 无聊的 wú liáo de

botanical garden 植物园 zhí wù yuán

bother v 打扰 dǎ rǎo

bottle 瓶 píng

bottle opener 瓶启子 píng qǐ zi

bowl 碗 wǎn

box 箱子 xiāng zi

boxing match 拳击比赛 quán jī bǐ sài

boy 男孩 nán hái

boyfriend 男朋友 nán péng you

bra 胸罩 xiōng zhào

bracelet 手镯 shǒu zhuó

brakes (car) 闸 zhá

break v **(tooth)** 断 duàn

break-in (burglary) 闯入 chuǎng rù

breakdown 出故障 chū gù zhàng

breakfast 早餐 zǎo cān

breast 乳房 rǔ fáng

breastfeed 母乳喂养 mǔ rǔ wèi yǎng

breathe v 呼吸 hū xī

bridge 桥梁 qiáo liáng

briefs (clothing) 男内裤 nán nèi kù

bring v 带来 dài lái

British 英国人 yīng guó rén

broken 破了 pò le

brooch 别针 bié zhēn

broom 笤帚 tiáo zhou

brother 兄弟 xiōng dì

brown 褐色 hè sè

bug 虫子 chóng zi

building 大厦 dà shà

burn v 烧 shāo

bus 公共汽车 gōng gòng qì chē

bus station 公共汽车站 gōng gòng qì chē zhàn

bus stop 公共汽车站 gōng g qì chē zhàn

bus ticket 公共汽车票 gōng gòng qì chē piào

bus tour 公共汽车游览 gōn gòng qì chē yóu lǎn

business 商务 shāng wù

business card 名片 míng piàn

business center 商业中心 sh yè zhōng xīn

business class 商务舱 shāng v cāng

business hours 营业时间 yín yè shí jiān

butcher 屠户 tú hù

buttocks 屁股 pì gu

buy v 买 mǎi

bye 再见 zài jiàn

C

cabin 客舱 kè cāng

cable car 缆车 lǎn chē

café 小餐馆 xiǎo cān guǎn

call v 打电话 dǎ diàn huà; ~ n 话 diàn huà

calligraphy supplies 书法用品 shū fǎ yòng pǐn

calories 卡路里 kǎ lù lǐ

camera 照相机 zhào xiàng jī

camera case 照相机套 zhào xiàng jī tào

mera store 照相器材商店
zhào xiàng qì cái shāng diàn

mp v 露营 lù yíng

mping stove 露营炉 lù yíng lú

mpsite 露营地 lù yíng dì

n opener 开罐器 kāi guàn qì

nada 加拿大 jiā ná dà

nadian 加拿大人 jiā ná dà
én

ncel v 取消 qǔ xiāo

ndy 糖果 táng guǒ

nned good 罐装食品 guàn
zhuāng shí pǐn

nyon 峡谷 xiá gǔ

r 汽车 qì chē

r hire [BE] 租车 zū chē

r park [BE] 停车场 tíng chē
chǎng

r rental 租车 chū zū qì chē

r seat (儿童) 车座 (ér tóng)
chē zuò

rafe 玻璃调料瓶 bō li tiáo
iào píng

rd 卡 kǎ

rry-on 手提行李 shǒu tí
xíng li

rt (grocery store) 手推车 shǒu
tuī chē; ~ **(luggage)** 行李推车
xíng li tuī chē

rton 条 tiáo

se (amount) 件 jiàn

cash v 兑现金 duì xiàn jīn; ~ n 现
金 xiàn jīn

cash advance 预支现金 yù zhī
xiàn jīn

cashier 出纳员 chū nà yuán

casino 赌博娱乐场 dǔ bó yú lè
chǎng

castle 城堡 chéng bǎo

cathedral 大教堂 dà jiào táng

cave 洞 dòng

CD CD CD

cell phone 手机 shǒu jī

Celsius 摄氏 shè shì

centimeter 厘米 lí mǐ

ceramic spoon 汤勺 tāng sháo

certificate 证明 zhèng míng

chair 椅子 yǐ zi

chair lift 升降椅 shēng jiàng yǐ

change v **(buses)** 换车 huàn chē;
~ v **(money)** 换钱 huàn qián; ~ v
(baby) 换尿布 huàn niào bù; ~ n
(money) 零钱 líng qián

charcoal 木炭 mù tàn

charge v **(credit card)** 用信用卡
付款 yòng xìn yòng kǎ fù kuǎn; **n**
(cost) 收费 shōu fèi

cheap 便宜 pián yi

cheaper 更便宜 gèng pián yi

check v **(something)** 检查 jiǎn
chá; ~ v **(luggage)** 托运 tuō yùn;
~ n **(payment)** 支票 zhī piào

check-in (hotel) 办入住 bàn rù zhù; **~ (airport)** 办理登机手续 bàn lǐ dēng jī shǒu xù

checking account 支票账户 zhī piào zhàng hù

check-out (hotel) *n* 退房 tuì fáng

chemical toilet 简易厕所 jiǎn yì cè suǒ

chemist *[BE]* 药剂师 yào jì shī

cheque *[BE]* 支票 zhī piào

chest (body part) 胸口 xiōng kǒu

chest pain 胸口痛 xiōng kǒu tòng

chewing gum 口香糖 kǒu xiāng táng

child 孩子 hái zi

child's seat 儿童座椅 ér tóng zuò yǐ

children's menu 儿童菜单 ér tóng cài dān

children's portion 儿童饭量 ér tóng fàn liàng

china 瓷器 cí qì

China 中国 zhōng guó

Chinese 中文 zhōng wén

Chinese painting 中国画 zhōng guó huà

chopsticks 筷子 kuài zi

church 教堂 jiào táng

cigar 雪茄 xuě jiā

cigarette 香烟 xiāng yān

class 等级 děng jí

clay pot 砂锅 shā guō

cloisonné 景泰蓝 jǐng tài lán

classical music 古典音乐 gǔ yīn yuè

clean *v* 清洗 qīng xǐ; **~ adv** 干 gān jìng

cleaning product 清洁产品 jié chǎn pǐn

cleaning supplies 清洁产品 应 qīng jié chǎn pǐn gōng yìng

clear *v* **(on an ATM)** 清除 qīng

cliff 峭壁 qiào bì

cling film *[BE]* 保鲜膜 bǎo xiā mó

close *v* **(a shop)** 关门 guān mé **adj** 近 jìn

closed 关闭 guān bì

clothing 衣物 yī wù

clothing store 服装店 fú zhuā diàn

club 俱乐部 jù lè bù

coat 外套 wài tào

coffee shop 咖啡店 kā fēi diàn

coin 硬币 yìng bì

cold (sickness) 感冒 gǎn mào; **(temperature)** 冷 lěng

colleague 同事 tóng shì

cologne 科隆香水 kē lóng xiā shuǐ

color 颜色 yán sè

comb 梳子 shū zi

me v 来 lái

mplaint 怨言 yuàn yán

mputer 计算机 jì suàn jī

ncert 音乐会 yīn yuè huì

ncert hall 音乐厅 yīn yuè tīng

ndition (medical) 症状 zhèng zhuàng

nditioner 护发素 hù fà sù

ndom 避孕套 bì yùn tào

nference 会议 huì yì

nfirm v 证实 zhèng shí

ngestion 充血 chōng xuè

nnect v (internet) 连接 lián jiē

nnection (internet) 连接 lián jiē; ~ (flight) 转机 zhuǎn jī

nstipated 便秘 biàn mì

nsulate 领事馆 lǐng shì guǎn

nsultant 顾问 gù wèn

ntact v 联系 lián xì

ntact lens 隐形眼镜 yǐn xíng ǎn jìng

ntact lens solution 隐形眼镜 夜 yǐn xíng yǎn jìng yè

ntagious 传染的 chuán rǎn de

nvention hall 会议厅 huì yì īng

nveyor belt 传送带 chuán òng dài

ok v 烹调 pēng tiáo

oking gas 烹调煤气 pēng tiáo néi qì

cool (temperature) 凉 liáng

copper 铜 tóng

corkscrew 开塞钻 kāi sāi zuàn

cost v 花费 huā fèi

cot 轻便小床 qīng biàn xiǎo chuáng

cotton 棉花 mián hua

cough 咳嗽 ké sou

country code 国家代号 guó jiā dài hào

cover charge 附加费 fù jiā fèi

crash v (car) 撞 zhuàng

cream (ointment) 药膏 yào gāo

credit card 信用卡 xìn yòng kǎ

crew neck 圆领 yuán lǐng

crib 摇篮 yáo lán

crystal 水晶 shuǐ jīng

cup 杯子 bēi zi

currency 货币 huò bì

currency exchange 货币兑换 huò bì duì huàn

currency exchange office 货币 兑换局 huò bì duì huàn jú

current account [BE] 支票账户 zhī piào zhàng hù

customs 海关 hǎi guān

cut v (hair) 剪 jiǎn; ~ n (injury) 伤口 shāng kǒu

cute 逗人喜爱 dòu rén xǐ ài

cycling 骑自行车 qí zì xíng chē

D

damage *v* 损伤 sǔn shāng

damaged 坏了 huài le

dance *v* 跳舞 tiào wǔ

dance club 舞蹈俱乐部 wǔ dǎo jù lè bù

dancing 跳舞 tiào wǔ

dangerous 危险 wēi xiǎn

dark 黑暗 hēi àn

date (calendar) 日期 rì qī

day 天 tiān

deaf 聋 lóng

debit card 借记卡 jiè jì kǎ

deck chair 轻便折叠躺椅 qīng biàn zhé dié tǎng yǐ

declare *v* 申报 shēn bào

decline *v* **(credit card)** 拒绝 jù jué

deeply 深深地 shēn shēn de

degrees (temperature) 度 dù

delay *v* 晚点 wǎn diǎn

delete *v* 删除 shān chú

delicatessen 熟食 shú shí

delicious 可口 kě kǒu

denim 斜纹粗棉布 xié wén cū mián bù

dentist 牙医 yá yī

denture 假牙 jiǎ yá

deodorant 止汗露 zhǐ hàn lù

department store 百货商店 bǎi huò shāng diàn

departure 离开 lí kāi

deposit *v* 存钱 cún qián; ~ *n* **(bank)** 储蓄 chǔ xù

desert 沙漠 shā mò

detergent 洗涤剂 xǐ dí jì

diabetic 糖尿病 táng niào bìng

dial *v* 拨号 bō hào

diamond 钻石 zuàn shí

diaper 尿布 niào bù

diarrhea 腹泻 fù xiè

diesel 柴油 chái yóu

difficult 困难 kùn nan

digital 数码 shù mǎ

digital camera 数码相机 shù mǎ xiàng jī

digital photo 数码相片 shù mǎ xiàng piàn

digital print 数码印刷品 shù mǎ yìn shuā pǐn

dining room 餐厅 cān tīng

dinner 晚餐 wǎn cān

direction 方向 fāng xiàng

dirty 肮脏 āng zāng

disabled 残疾 cán jí

disabled accessible *[BE]* 残疾人通道 cán jí rén tōng dào

disconnect (computer) 断开 duàn kāi

discount 折扣 zhé kòu

dish (kitchen) 碟子 dié zi

dishwasher 洗碗机 xǐ wǎn jī

washing liquid 洗碗液 xǐ wǎn yè

display 显示 xiǎn shì

display case 陈列橱 chén liè chú

disposable 一次性 yí cì xìng

disposable razor 一次性剃刀 yí cì xìng tì dāo

dive v 潜水 qián shuǐ

diving equipment 潜水用具 qián shuǐ yòng jù

divorce v 离婚 lí hūn

dizzy 头昏眼花 tóu hūn yǎn huā

doctor 医生 yī shēng

doll 玩具娃娃 wán jù wá wá

dollar (U.S.) 美元 měi yuán

domestic 国内 guó nèi

domestic flight 国内航班 guó nèi háng bān

dormitory 宿舍 sù shè

double bed 双人床 shuāng rén chuáng

downtown 市中心 shì zhōng xīn

dozen 十二 shí èr

drag lift 牵引缆车 qiān yǐn lǎn chē

dress (piece of clothing) 连衣裙 lián yī qún

dress code 着装要求 zhuó zhuāng yāo qiú

drink v 喝 hē; ~ n 饮料 yǐn liào

drink menu 饮料单 yǐn liào dān

drinking water 饮用水 yǐn yòng shuǐ

drive v 开车 kāi chē

driver's license number 司机驾照号 sī jī jià zhào hào

drop (medicine) 滴 dī

drowsiness 睡意 shuì yì

dry cleaner 干洗店 gān xǐ diàn

during 期间 qī jiān

duty (tax) 关税 guān shuì

duty-free 免税 miǎn shuì

DVD DVD DVD

E

ear 耳朵 ěr duo

earache 耳朵疼 ěr duo téng

early 早 zǎo

earrings 耳环 ěr huán

east 东部 dōng bù

easy 容易 róng yì

eat v 吃 chī

economy class 经济舱 jīng jì cāng

elbow 肘 zhǒu

electric outlet 电插座 diàn chā zuò

elevator 电梯 diàn tī

e-mail v 发电邮 fā diàn yóu; ~ n 电子邮件 diàn zǐ yóu jiàn

e-mail address 电邮地址 diàn yóu dì zhǐ

emergency 紧急状态 jǐn jí
zhuàng tài

emergency exit 紧急出口 jǐn jí
chū kǒu

empty v 倒空 dào kōng

enamel (jewelry) 珐琅 fà láng

end v 结束 jié shù

English 英语 yīng yǔ

engrave v 雕刻 diāo kè

enjoy v 享用 xiǎng yòng

enter v 进入 jìn rù

entertainment 娱乐 yú lè

entrance 入口 rù kǒu

envelope 信封 xìn fēng

epileptic 癫痫 diān xián

equipment 设备 shè bèi

escalator 自动扶梯 zì dòng fú tī

e-ticket 电子票 diàn zǐ piào

evening 晚上 wǎn shang

excess 超过 chāo guò

exchange v **(money)** 兑换 duì
huàn; ~ v **(goods)** 交换 jiāo
huàn; ~ n **(place)** 换地方 huàn
dì fāng

exchange rate 兑换率 duì huàn
lǜ

excursion 游览 yóu lǎn

excuse v 原谅 yuán liàng

exhausted 用尽 yòng jìn

exit v 出去 chū qù; ~ n 出口 chū
kǒu

expensive 昂贵 ang guì

expert (skill level) 专家 zh
jiā

exposure (film) 曝光 bào gu

express 快 kuài

extension (phone) 分机 fēn

extra 额外 é wài

extra large 特大号 tè dà hàc

extract v **(tooth)** 拔 bá

eye 眼睛 yǎn jīng

F

face 面孔 miàn kǒng

facial 面部 miàn bù

family 家庭 jiā tíng

fan (appliance) 电扇 diàn sh

far 远 yuǎn

far-sighted 远视 yuǎn shì

farm 农场 nóng chǎng

fast 快速 kuài sù

fast food 快餐 kuài cān

fat free 无脂肪 wú zhī fáng

father 父亲 fù qīn

fax v 发传真 fā chuán zhēn; ~
传真 chuán zhēn

fax number 传真号 chuán zł
hào

fee 费用 fèi yòng

feed v 喂 wèi

ferry 轮渡 lún dù

fever 发烧 fā shāo

ld (sports) 运动场 yùn dòng hǎng

up v (food) 加满 jiā mǎn

out v (form) 填写 tián xiě

ling (tooth) 填充物 tián chōng vù

m (camera) 胶卷 jiāo juǎn

e (fee) 罚款 fá kuǎn

ger 手指 shǒu zhǐ

gernail 指甲 zhǐ jiǎ

e 火 huǒ

e department 消防队 xiāo áng duì

e door 防火门 fáng huǒ mén

st class 头等舱 tóu děng cāng

(clothing) 适合 shì hé

ting room 试衣间 shì yī jiān

v **(repair)** 修理 xiū lǐ

ed-price menu 价格固定的菜单 jià gé gù dìng de cài dān

shlight 手电 shǒu diàn

ght 航班 háng bān

or 地板 dì bǎn

rist 卖花人 mài huā rén

wer 花 huā

lk music 民间音乐 mín jiān yīn yuè

od 食物 shí wù

ot 脚 jiǎo

otball game [BE] 足球赛 zú qiú sài

for 为 wéi

forecast 预报 yù bào

forest 森林 sēn lín

fork 叉子 chā zi

form (fill-in) 表格 biǎo gé

formula (baby) 奶粉 nǎi fěn

fort 要塞 yào sài

fountain 喷泉 pēn quán

free 免费 miǎn fèi

freezer 冷冻机 lěng dòng jī

fresh 新鲜 xīn xiān

friend 朋友 péng you

frying pan 煎锅 jiān guō

full-service 全面服务 quán miàn fú wù

G

game 游戏 yóu xì

garage 车库 chē kù

garbage bag 垃圾袋 lā jī dài

gas 汽油 qì yóu

gas station 加油站 jiā yóu zhàn

gate (airport) 登机门 dēng jī mén

gay 男同性恋 nán tóng xìng liàn

gay bar 男同性恋酒吧 nán tóng xìng liàn jiǔ bā

gay club 男同性恋俱乐部 nán tóng xìng liàn jù lè bù

gel (hair) 发胶 fà jiāo

get to 到 dào

get off (a train/bus/subway) 下车 xià chē

gift 礼物 lǐ wù

gift shop 礼品店 lǐ pǐn diàn

girl 女孩 nǚ hái

girlfriend 女朋友 nǚ péng you

give v 给 gěi

glass (drinking) 玻璃杯 bō li bēi; **~ (material)** 玻璃 bō li

glasses 眼镜 yǎn jìng

go v **(somewhere)** 去 qù

gold 金子 jīn zi

golf course 高尔夫球场 gāo ěr fū qiú chǎng

golf tournament 高尔夫球比赛 gāo ěr fū qiú bǐ sài

good 好 hǎo

good afternoon 下午好 xià wu hǎo

good evening 晚上好 wǎn shang hǎo

good morning 早晨好 zǎo chen hǎo

goodbye 再见 zài jiàn

goods 物品 wù pǐn

gram 克 kè

grandchild 孙子 sūn zi

grandparent 祖父／母 zǔ fù/mǔ

gray 灰色 huī sè

Great Hall of the People 人民大会堂 rén mín dà huì táng

green 绿色 lnǜ sè

grocery store 杂货店 zá huò

ground floor 一楼 yī lóu

group 小组 xiǎo zǔ

guide n 指南 zhǐ nán

guide book 指南书 zhǐ nán sh

guide dog 导盲犬 dǎo máng quǎn

gym 体操 tǐ cāo

gynecologist 妇产科医师 fù chǎn kē yī shī

H

hair 头发 tóu fà

hair dryer 吹风机 chuī fēng jī

hair salon 发廊 fà láng

hairbrush 梳子 shū zi

haircut 理发 lǐ fà

hairspray 喷发剂 pēn fà jì

hairstyle 发型 fà xíng

hairstylist 发型师 fà xíng shī

halal 清真食品 qīng zhēn shí

half 半 bàn

half hour 半小时 bàn xiǎo shí

half-kilo 半公斤 bàn gōng jīn

hammer 锤子 chuí zi

hand 手 shǒu

hand luggage [BE] 手提行李 shǒu tí xíng li

handbag [BE] 提包 tí bāo

handicapped 残疾 cán ji

handicapped-accessible 残疾人通道 cán jí rén tōng dào

hangover 宿醉 sù zuì

happy 愉快 yú kuài

hat 帽子 mào zi

have v 有 yǒu

hay fever 花粉症 huā fěn zhèng

head (body part) 头 tóu

headache 头疼 tóu téng

headphones 耳机 ěr jī

health 健康 jiàn kāng

health food store 健康食品商店 jiàn kāng shí pǐn shāng diàn

hearing impaired 听力障碍 tīng lì zhàng ài

heart 心脏 xīn zàng

heart condition 心脏病 xīn zàng bìng

heat 暖气 nuǎn qì

heater 加热器 jiā rè qì

heating [BE] 暖气 nuǎn qì

hello 你好 nǐ hǎo

helmet 头盔 tóu kuī

help 帮助 bāng zhù

here 这里 zhè lǐ

你好 nǐ hǎo

high 高 gāo

highchair 高脚椅 gāo jiǎo yǐ

highway 高速公路 gāo sù gōng lù

hill 小山 xiǎo shān

hire v [BE] 雇用 gù yòng

hire car [BE] 租用汽车 zū yòng qì chē

hitchhike v 搭车 dā chē

hockey 曲棍球 qū gùn qiú

holiday [BE] 假日 jià rì

horse track 跑马场 pǎo mǎ chǎng

hospital 医院 yī yuàn

hostel 旅舍 lǚ shè

hot (temperature) 热 rè; ~ (spicy) 辣 là

hot spring 温泉 wēn quán

hot water 热水 rè shuǐ

hotel 旅馆 lǚ guǎn

hour 小时 xiǎo shí

house 房子 fáng zi

household good 家用物品 jiā yòng

housekeeping services 客房清洁服务 kè fáng qīng jié fú wù

how 怎么 zěn me

how much 多少 duō shǎo

hug v 拥抱 yōng bào

hungry 饥饿 jī è

hurt 疼 téng

husband 丈夫 zhàng fu

I

ibuprofen 布洛芬 bù luò fēn

ice 冰 bīng

ice hockey 冰球 bīng qiú

icy 冰冷 bīng lěng
identification 证件 zhèng jiàn
ill 病 bìng
in 在 zài
include v 包括 bāo kuò
indoor pool 室内游泳池 shì nèi yóu yǒng chí
inexpensive 不贵 bú guì
infected 传染 chuán rǎn
information (phone) 留言 liú yán
information desk 问讯处 wèn xùn chù
insect bite 虫咬 chóng yǎo
insect repellent 杀虫剂 shā chóng jì
insert v (on an ATM) 插入 chā rù
insomnia 失眠 shī mián
instant message 即时讯息 jí shí xùn xī
insulin 胰岛素 yí dǎo sù
insurance 保险 bǎo xiǎn
insurance card 保险卡 bǎo xiǎn kǎ
insurance company 保险公司 bǎo xiǎn gōng sī
interesting 有趣 yǒu qù
international (airport area) 国际 guó jì
international flight 国际航班 guó jì háng bān

international student card 国学生证 guó jì xué shēng zhèn
internet 互联网 hù lián wǎng
internet cafe 网吧 wǎng bā
internet service 互联网服务 lián wǎng fú wù
interpreter 口译员 kǒu yì yuá
intersection 十字路口 shí zì lù kǒu
intestine 肠子 cháng zi
introduce v 介绍 jiè shào
invoice 发货票 fā huò piào
Ireland 爱尔兰 ài ěr lán
Irish 爱尔兰人 ài ěr lán rén
iron v 熨衣服 yùn yī fu; ~ n 熨 yùn dǒu

J

jacket 夹克 jiá kè
jade 翡翠 fěi cuì
Japanese (restaurant) 日本 rì
jar 罐子 guàn zi
jaw 下颌 xià hé
jazz 爵士乐 jué shì yuè
jazz club 爵士乐俱乐部 jué yuè jù lè bù
jeans 牛仔裤 niú zǎi kù
jeweler 珠宝商 zhū bǎo shāng
jewelry 首饰 shǒu shì
join v 加入 jiā rù
joint (body part) 关节 guān jié

钥匙 yào shi

card 钥匙卡 yào shi kǎ

ring 钥匙圈 yào shi quān

die pool 儿童游泳池 ér tóng

u yǒng chí

ney (body part) 肾脏 shèn

ng

gram 公斤 gōng jīn

meter 公里 gōng lǐ

v 亲吻 qīn wěn

hen 厨房 chú fáng

hen foil [BE] 厨房锡纸 chú

ng xī zhǐ

e 膝盖 xī gài

fe 刀子 dāo zi

her 犹太食品 yóu tài shí pǐn

e 鞋带 xié dài

querware 漆器 qī qì

tose intolerant 乳糖过敏 rǔ

ing guò mǐn

e 湖 hú

ge 大 dà

t 最后 zuì hòu

e (time) 晚了 wǎn le

er 以后 yǐ hòu

nderette [BE] 洗衣店 xǐ yī diàn

ndromat 洗衣店 xǐ yī diàn

ndry 要洗的衣物 yào xǐ de

yī wù

laundry facility 洗衣店设施 xǐ

yī diàn shè shī

laundry service 洗衣服务 xǐ yī

fú wù

lawyer 律师 lǜ shī

leather 皮革 pí gé

leave v 起飞 qǐ fēi

left (direction) 左边 zuǒ bian

leg 腿 tuǐ

lens 镜片 jìng piàn

less 较少 jiào shǎo

lesson 课程 kè chéng

letter 信件 xìn jiàn

library 图书馆 tú shū guǎn

life jacket 救生衣 jiù shēng yī

lifeguard 救生员 jiù shēng yuán

lift 搭车 dā chē; ~ [BE] 电梯

diàn tī

lift pass 缆车票 lǎn chē piào

light (overhead) 灯 dēng; ~

(cigarette) 点 diǎn

lightbulb 电灯泡 diàn dēng pào

lighter 打火机 dǎ huǒ jī

like v 喜欢 xǐ huan

line (train) 线 xiàn

linen 亚麻布 yà má bù

lip 嘴唇 zuǐ chún

liquor store 酒店 jiǔ diàn

liter 公升 gōng shēng

little 少许 shǎo xǔ

live v 居住 jū zhù

live music 现场音乐 xiàn chǎng yīn yuè

liver (body part) 肝脏 gān zàng

loafers 游荡者 yóu dàng zhě

local 当地 dāng dì

lock up 锁锁 suǒ

lock n 锁 suǒ

locker 衣物柜 yī wù guì

log on 登录 dēng lù

log off 退出 tuì chū

long 长 cháng

long sleeves 长袖子 cháng xiù zi

long-sighted [BE] 远视 yuǎn shì

look v 看 kàn

lose v (something) 丢失 diū shī

lost 失去 shī qù

lost and found 失物招领处 shī wù zhāo lǐng chù

lotion 化妆乳液 huà zhuāng rǔ yè

louder 大声 dà shēng

love 爱 ài

low 低 dī

luggage 行李 xíng li

luggage cart 行李推车 xíng li tuī chē

luggage locker 行李暂存箱 xíng li zàn cún xiāng

luggage ticket 行李票 xíng li piào

lunch 午餐 wǔ cān

lung 肺 fèi

M

magazine 杂志 zá zhì

magnificent 壮观 zhuàng guā

mail v 邮寄 yóu jì; ~ n 邮件 y jiàn

mailbox 邮箱 yóu xiāng

main attraction 主要景点 z yào jǐng diǎn

main course 主菜 zhǔ cài

make up v [BE] (a prescription 药方 pèi yào fāng

mall 购物中心 gòu wù zhōng

man 男人 nán rén

manager 经理 jīng lǐ

manicure 修手指甲 xiū shǒu zhi jia

manual car 手动汽车 shǒu d qì chē

map n 地图 dì tú

market 市场 shì chǎng

married 结婚 jié hūn

marry v 结婚 jié hūn

mass (church service) 礼拜 lǐ

massage 按摩 àn mó

match n 火柴 huǒ chái

meal 饭 fàn

measure v (someone) 测量 c liáng

measuring cup 量杯 liáng bēi

measuring spoon 量匙 liáng chí

mechanic 技工 jì gōng

medicine 医药 yī yào

medium (size) 中等 zhōng děng

meet v (someone) 见面 jiàn miàn

meeting 会议 huì yì

meeting room 会议室 huì yì shì

membership card 会员证 huì yuán zhèng

memorial (place) 纪念馆 jì niàn guǎn

memory card 存储卡 cún chǔ kǎ

mend v 修理 xiū lǐ

menstrual cramp 经期腹痛 jīng qī fù tòng

menu 菜单 cài dān

message 信息 xìn xī

meter (parking) 计时器 jì shí qì

microwave 微波炉 wēi bō lú

midday [BE] 午间 wǔ jiān

midnight 午夜 wǔ yè

mileage 里程（数）lǐ chéng shù

mini-bar 小酒吧 xiǎo jiǔ bā

minute 分钟 fēn zhōng

missing 错过 cuò guò

mistake 差错 chā cuò

mobile phone [BE] 手机 shǒu jī

mobility 流动性 liú dòng xìng

monastery 修道院 xiū dào yuàn

money 钱 qián

month 月 yuè

mop 擦 cā

moped 电动自行车 diàn dòng zì xíng chē

more 更多 gèng duō

morning 早晨 zǎo chén

mosque 清真寺 qīng zhēn sì

mother 母亲 mǔ qīn

motion sickness 晕动病 yùn dòng bìng

motor boat 汽船 qì chuán

motorcycle 摩托车 mó tuō chē

motorway [BE] 高速公路 gāo sù gōng lù

mountain 山 shān

mountain bike 山地车 shān dì chē

mousse (hair) 摩丝 mó sī

mouth 嘴 zuǐ

movie 电影 diàn yǐng

movie theater 电影院 diàn yǐng yuàn

mug v 抢 qiǎng

multiple-trip (ticket) 不限使用次数的 bú xiàn shǐ yòng cì shù de

muscle 肌肉 jī ròu

museum 博物馆 bó wù guǎn

music 音乐 yīn yuè

music store 音乐商店 yīn yuè shāng diàn

N

nail file 指甲锉 zhǐ jia cuò

nail salon 美甲沙龙 měi jiǎ shā lóng

name 名字 míng zì

napkin 餐巾 cān jīn

nappy [BE] 尿布 niào bù

nationality 国籍 guó jí

nature preserve 自然保护区 zì rán bǎo hù qū

nauseous 恶心 ě xin

near (在...的)附近 (zài... de) fù jìn

near-sighted 近视 jìn shì

nearby 附近 fù jìn

neck 脖子 bó zǐ

necklace 项链 xiàng liàn

need v 需要 xū yào

newspaper 报纸 bào zhǐ

newsstand 报摊 bào tān

next 下一个 xià yí gè

nice 好 hǎo

night 夜 yè

nightclub 夜总会 yè zǒng huì

no 不 bú/bù

non-alcoholic 无酒精 wú jiǔ jīng

non-smoking 禁烟 jìn yān

noon 中午 zhōng wǔ

north 北部 běi bù

nose 鼻子 bí zi

notes [BE] 笔记 bǐ jì

nothing 没什么 méi shén me

notify v 通知 tōng zhī

novice (skill level) 新手 xīn shǒu

now 现在 xiàn zài

number 数字 shù zì

nurse 护士 hù shi

O

office 办公室 bàn gōng shì

office hours 办公时间 bàn gōng shí jiān

off-licence [BE] 酒店 jiǔ diàn

oil 油 yóu

OK 好 hǎo

old 老 lǎo

on the corner 在拐角处 zài guǎi jiǎo chù

once 一次 yí cì

one 一 yī

one-way (ticket) 单程 dān chéng

one-way street 单行道 dān xíng dào

only 只 zhǐ

open v 打开 dǎ kāi; ~ adj 开着 kāi zhe

opera 歌剧 gē jù

opera house 歌剧院 gē jù yuàn

opposite 相反 xiāng fǎn

optician 验光师 yàn guāng shī

orange (color) 桔色 jú sè

orchestra 乐队 yuè duì

...der v 点菜 diǎn cài

...tdoor pool 室外游泳池 shì
...wài yóu yǒng chí

...tside 外面 wài miàn

...er the counter (medication) 非
...处方药 fēi chǔ fāng yào

...erdone 过熟 guò shú

...erlook (scenic place) 俯视 fǔ shì

...ernight 隔夜 gé yè

...ygen treatment 氧气治疗
...ǎng qì zhì liáo

...n. 下午 xià wǔ

...cifier 橡皮奶嘴 xiàng pí nǎi zuǐ

...ck v 打包 dǎ bāo

...ckage 包裹 bāo guǒ

...ddling pool [BE] 儿童游泳池
...r tóng yóu yǒng chí

...d [BE] 垫 diàn

...in 痛 tòng

...jamas 睡衣 shuì yī

...lace 宫殿 gōng diàn

...nts 裤子 kù zi

...ntyhose 裤袜 kù wà

...per 纸 zhǐ

...per towel 纸巾 zhǐ jīn

...racetamol [BE] 泰诺 tài nuò

...rk v 停车 tíng chē; ~ n 公园
...gōng yuán

...rking garage 车库 chē kù

parking lot 停车场 tíng chē chǎng

parking meter 停车计时器 tíng
chē jì shí qì

part (for car) 部件 bù jiàn

part-time 兼职 jiān zhí

passenger 乘客 chéng kè

passport 护照 hù zhào

passport control 护照管制 hù
zhào guǎn zhì

password 密码 mì mǎ

pastry shop 点心店 diǎn xīn diàn

path 道路 dào lù

pay v 支付 zhī fù

pay phone 公用电话 gōng yòng
diàn huà

peak (of a mountain) 山顶 shān
dǐng

pearl 珍珠 zhēn zhū

pedestrian 行人 xíng rén

pediatrician 儿科医生 ér kē yī
shēng

pedicure 修脚趾甲 xiū jiǎo zhǐ jiǎ

pen 笔 bǐ

penicillin 青霉素 qīng méi sù

penis 阴茎 yīn jīng

per 每 měi

per day 每天 měi tiān

per hour 每小时 měi xiǎo shí

per night 每晚 měi wǎn

per week 每星期 měi xīng qī

perfume 香水 xiāng shuǐ

period (menstrual) 月经 yuè jīng;
~**(of time)** 期间 qī jiān

permit v 允许 yǔn xǔ

petite 娇小 jiāo xiǎo

petrol [BE] 汽油 qì yóu

petrol station [BE] 加油站 jiā
yóu zhàn

pharmacy 药房 yào fáng

phone v 打电话 dǎ diàn huà; ~ n
电话 diàn huà

phone call 电话 diàn huà

phone card 电话卡 dǎ diàn kǎ

phone number 电话号码 diàn
huà hào mǎ

photo 相片 xiàng piàn

photocopy 复印件 fù yìn jiàn

photography 摄影 shè yǐng

pick up (something) 取 qǔ

picnic area 野餐区 yě cān qū

piece 片 piàn

pill (birth control) 计划生育药
片 jì huà shēng yù yào piàn

pillow 枕头 zhěn tou

**personal identification number
(PIN)** 个人密码 gè rén mì mǎ

pink 粉红色 fěn hóng sè

piste [BE] 小道 xiǎo dào

piste map [BE] 小道路线图 xiǎo
dào lù xiàn tú

pizzeria 比萨店 bǐ sà diàn

place v **(a bet)** 下 xià

plane 飞机 fēi jī

plastic wrap 塑料包装 sù liào
bāo zhuāng

plate 盘子 pán zi

platform 站台 zhàn tái

platinum 铂金 bó jīn

play v 玩 wán; ~ n **(theatre)** 戏
剧 xì jù

playground 操场 cāo chǎng

playpen 游戏围栏 yóu xì wéi
lán

please 请 qǐng

pleasure 乐趣 lè qù

plunger 下水道疏通器 xià
dào shū tōng qì

plus size 加大号 jiā dà hào

pocket 口袋 kǒu dài

poison 毒药 dú yào

poles (skiing) 滑雪杆 huá xuě
gan

police 警察 jǐng chá

police report 警察报告 jǐng chá
bào gào

police station 警察局 jǐng chá jú

pond 池塘 chí táng

pool 水池 shuǐ chí

pop music 流行音乐 liú xíng
yīn yuè

portion 部分 bù fen

post [BE] 邮件 yóu jiàn

post office 邮局 yóu jú

stbox [BE] 邮箱 yóu xiāng

stcard 明信片 míng xìn piàn

罐 guàn

ttery 陶器 táo qì

und (weight) 磅 bàng; ~

British sterling) 英镑 yīng
àng

gnant 怀孕 huái yùn

scribe v 开处方 kāi chǔ fāng

scription 处方药 chǔ fāng
ào

ss v (clothing) 熨 yùn

ce 价格 jià gé

nt v 打印 dǎ yìn

blem 问题 wèn tí

duce 农产品 nóng chǎn pǐn

duce store 农产品商店
óng chǎn pǐn shāng diàn

hibit v 禁止 jìn zhǐ

nounce v 发音 fā yīn

blic 公共 gōng gòng

l v 拉 lā

rple 紫色 zǐ sè

rse 提包 tí bāo

sh v 按 àn

shchair [BE] 婴儿车 yīng ér chē

ality 质量 zhì liàng

estion 问题 wèn tí

et 安静 ān jìng

R

racetrack 跑马场 pǎo mǎ chǎng

racket (sports) 球拍 qiú pāi

railway station [BE] 火车 huǒ
chē

rain n 雨 yǔ

raincoat 雨衣 yǔ yī

rainforest 雨林 yǔ lín

rainy 多雨 duō yǔ

rap (music) 说唱乐 shuō chàng
yuè

rape 强奸 qiáng jiān

rare (object) 罕见 hǎn jiàn

rash 皮疹 pí zhěn

ravine 峡谷 xiá gǔ

razor blade 剃须刀 tì xū dāo

reach v 够 gòu

ready 准备好 zhǔn bèi hǎo

real 真正 zhēn zhèng

receipt 收据 shōu jù

receive v 接受 jiē shòu

reception 招待会 zhāo dài huì

recharge v 充电 chōng diàn

recommend v 推荐 tuī jiàn

recommendation 推荐 tuī jiàn

recycling 回收 huí shōu

red 红色 hóng sè

refrigerator 冰箱 bīng xiāng

region 区域 qū yù

registered mail 挂号信 guà hào
xìn

regular 普通 pǔ tōng

relationship 关系 guān xì

Ren Min Bi 人民币 rén mín bì

rent v 租 zū

rental car 出租车 chū zū chē

repair v 修理 xiū lǐ

repeat v 重复 chóng fù

reservation 预定 yù dìng

reservation desk 服务台 fú wù tái

reserve v 预定 yù dìng

restaurant 餐馆 cān guǎn

restroom (formal/informal) 洗手间/厕所 xǐ shǒu jiān/cè suǒ

retired 退休 tuì xiū

return v 归还 guī huán; ~ n [BE] 返还 fǎn huán

reverse v (the charges) [BE] 对方付费电话 duì fāng fù fèi diàn huà

rib (body part) 肋骨 lèi gǔ

rice cooker 电饭锅 diàn fàn guō

right of way 路权 lù quán

ring 戒指 jiè zhi

river 河 hé

road map 路线图 lù xiàn tú

roast v 烤 kǎo

rob v 抢夺 qiǎng duó

robbed 被抢了 bèi qiǎng le

romantic 浪漫 làng màn

room 房间 fáng jiān

room key 房间钥匙 fáng jiān yào shi

room service 客房送餐服务 fáng sòng cān fú wù

round-trip 双程 shuāng chéng

route 路线 lù xiàn

rowboat 划艇 huá tǐng

rubbish [BE] 垃圾 lā jī

rubbish bag [BE] 垃圾袋 lā jī

ruins 废墟 fèi xū

rush 赶时间 gǎn shí jiān

S

sad 伤心 shāng xīn

safe (thing) 保险柜 bǎo xiǎn ~ (protected) 安全 ān quán

sales tax 销售税 xiāo shòu sh

sandals 凉鞋 liáng xié

sanitary napkin 卫生棉 wèi shēng mián

saucepan 平底锅 píng dǐ guō

sauna 蒸汽浴 zhēng qì yù

save v (on a computer) 保存 cún

savings (account) 储蓄 chǔ x

scanner 扫描器 sǎo miáo qì

scarf 围巾 wéi jīn

schedule v 预定日程 yù dìng chéng; ~ n 日程表 rì chéng b

school 学校 xué xiào

science 科学 kē xué

issors 剪刀 jiǎn dāo

a 海 hǎi

at 座位 zuò wèi

curity 安检 ān jiǎn

e v 看见 kàn jiàn

lf-service 自助 zì zhù

ll v 卖 mài

minar 研讨会 yán tǎo huì

nd v 送 sòng

nior citizen 老年人 lǎo nián rén

parated (marriage) 分居 fēn jū

rious 严肃 yán sù

rvice (in a restaurant) 服务 fú wù

xually transmitted disease (STD) 性传播疾病 xìng chuán bō jí bìng

ampoo 香波 xiāng bō

arp 锋利 fēng lì

aving cream 剃须膏 tì xū gāo

eet 床单 chuáng dān

ip v **(mail)** 邮寄 yóu jì

irt 衬衫 chèn shān

oe store 鞋店 xié diàn

oes 鞋子 xié zi

op v 购物 gòu wù

opping 购物 gòu wù

opping area 购物区 gòu wù qū

opping centre [BE] 购物中心 gòu wù zhōng xīn

opping mall 商城 shāng chéng

short 短小 duǎn xiǎo

short sleeves 短袖 duǎn xiù

shorts 短裤 duǎn kù

short-sighted [BE] 近视 jìn shì

shoulder 肩膀 jiān bǎng

show v 显示 xiǎn shì

shower 淋浴 lín yù

shrine 寺庙 sì miào

sick 病了 bìng le

side dish 配菜 pèi cài

side effect 副作用 fù zuò yòng

sightseeing 观光 guān guāng

sightseeing tour 观光旅游 guān guāng lǚ yóu

sign v 签字 qiān zì

silk 丝绸 sī chóu

silver 银 yín

single (unmarried) 单身 dān shēn

single bed 单人床 dān rén chuáng

single room 单人房间 dān rén fáng jiān

sink 水槽 shuǐ cáo

sister 姐妹 jiě mèi

sit v 坐下 zuò xià

size 尺寸 chǐ cùn

skin 皮肤 pí fū

skirt 裙子 qún zi

ski 滑雪 huá xuě

ski lift 滑雪缆车 huá xuě lǎn chē

sleep v 睡觉 shuì jiào

sleeper car 卧铺车 wò pù chē

sleeping bag 睡袋 shuì dài

sleeping car [BE] 卧铺车 wò pù chē

slice (of something) 切片 qiē piàn

slippers 拖鞋 tuō xié

slower 更慢 gèng màn

slowly 慢慢地 màn màn de

small 小 xiǎo

smaller 更小 gèng xiǎo

smoke v 吸烟 xī yān

smoking (area) 吸烟区 xī yān qū

snack bar 小吃店 xiǎo chī diàn

sneaker 运动鞋 yùn dòng xié

snorkeling equipment 水下呼吸设备 shuǐ xià hū xī shè bèi

snowboard 滑雪板 huá xuě bǎn

snowshoe 雪靴 xuě xuē

snowy 多雪 duō xuě

soap 肥皂 féi zào

soccer 足球 zú qiú

sock 袜子 wà zi

soother [BE] 橡皮奶嘴 xiàng pí nǎi zuǐ

sore throat 喉咙痛 hóu lóng tòng

sorry 抱歉 bào qiàn

south 南 nán

souvenir 纪念品 jì niàn pǐn

souvenir store 纪念品商店 jì niàn pǐn shāng diàn

spa 温泉 wēn quán

spatula 小铲子 xiǎo chǎn zi

speak v 讲话 jiǎng huà

specialist (doctor) 专家 zhuān

specimen 标本 biāo běn

speeding 超速开车 chāo sù k chē

spell v 拼写 pīn xiě

spicy 辣là

spine (body part) 脊椎 jǐ zhuī

spoon 勺子 sháo zi

sports 体育 tǐ yù

sporting goods store 体育用品商店 tǐ yù yòng pǐn shāng diàn

sports massage 体育按摩 tǐ àn mó

sprain 扭伤 niǔ shāng

stadium 体育场 tǐ yù chǎng

stairs 台阶 tái jiē

stamp v (a ticket) 盖印 gài yìn n (postage) 邮票 yóu piào

start v 开始 kāi shǐ

starter [BE] 开胃菜 kāi wèi cài

station 站 zhàn

statue 雕像 diāo xiàng

stay v 住在 zhù zài

steal v 偷 tōu

steamer 蒸锅 zhēng guō

steep 陡峭 dǒu qiào

sterling silver 纯银 chún yín

sting n 蜇 zhē

len 被偷了 bèi tōu le

mach 胃 wèi

machache 胃疼 wèi téng

p v 住手 zhù shǒu; ~ n 站
hàn

re directory 商店目录 shāng
iàn mù lù

rey [BE] 楼层 lóu céng

ve 炉子 lú zi

aight 直 zhí

ange 奇怪 qí guài

eam 小溪 xiǎo xī

oller 婴儿推车 yīng ér tuī chē

dent 学生 xué shēng

dy v 学习 xué xí

nning 震惊 zhèn jīng

btitle 副标题 fù biāo tí

bway 地铁 dì tiě

bway station 地铁站 dì tiě
hàn

it 西服套装 xī fú tào zhuāng

itcase 手提箱 shǒu tí xiāng

n 太阳 tài yáng

nblock 防晒霜 fáng shài
huāng

nburn 晒伤 shài shāng

nglasses 太阳镜 tài yáng jìng

nny 晴朗 qíng lǎng

nscreen 防晒霜 fáng shài
huāng

nstroke 中暑 zhòng shǔ

super (fuel) 超级 chāo jí

supermarket 超级市场 chāo jí
shì chǎng

supervision 监督 jiān dū

surfboard 冲浪板 chōng làng
bǎn

swallow v 吞下 tūn xià

sweater 毛衣 máo yī

sweatshirt 运动衫 yùn dòng
shān

sweet (taste) 甜 tián

sweets [BE] 甜点 tián diǎn

swelling 肿胀 zhǒng zhàng

swim v 游泳 yóu yǒng

swimsuit 游泳衣 yóu yǒng yī

symbol (keyboard) 标志 biāo zhì

synagogue 犹太教堂 yóu tài
jiào táng

T

table 桌子 zhuō zi

tablet (medicine) 片剂 piàn jì

take v 吃药 chī yào

take away [BE] 拿走 ná zǒu

tampon 月经栓 yuè jīng shuān

taste v 尝尝 cháng chang

taxi 出租车 chū zū chē

team 队 duì

teahouse 茶馆 chá guǎn

teaspoon 茶匙 chá chí

telephone 电话 diàn huà

temple (religious) 寺庙 sì miào

temporary 临时 lín shí

tennis 网球 wǎng qiú

tent 帐篷 zhàng péng

tent peg 帐蓬桩 zhàng péng zhuāng

tent pole 帐篷杆 zhàng péng gǎn

terminal (airport) 候机厅 hòu jī tīng

terracotta 赤土陶 chì tǔ táo

terrible 可怕 kě pà

text v **(send a message)** 发短信 fā duǎn xìn; ~ n **(message)** 文字 wén zì

thank v 感谢 gǎn xiè

thank you 谢谢 xiè xie

that 那 nà

theater 剧院 jù yuàn

theft 偷窃 tōu qiè

there 那里 nà li

thief 小偷 xiǎo tōu

thigh 大腿 dà tuǐ

thirsty 渴 kě

this 这 zhè

throat 喉咙 hóu lóng

thunderstorm 雷雨 léi yǔ

ticket 票 piào

ticket office 售票处 shòu piào chù

tie (clothing) 领带 lǐng dài

tights [BE] 裤袜 kù wà

time 时间 shí jiān

timetable [BE] 时间表 shí jiān biāo

tire 轮胎 lún tāi

tired 累了 lèi le

tissue 面巾纸 miàn jīn zhǐ

to go 拿走 ná zǒu

tobacconist 烟草零售商 yā líng shòu shāng

today 今天 jīn tiān

toe 脚趾 jiǎo zhǐ

toenail 脚趾甲 jiǎo zhǐ jia

toilet [BE] **(formal/informal)** 洗手间／厕所 xǐ shǒu jiān/cè s

toilet paper 卫生纸 wèi shēn zhǐ

tomorrow 明天 míng tiān

tongue 舌头 shé tou

tonight 今晚 jīn wǎn

too 太 tài

tooth 牙 yá

toothpaste 牙膏 yá gāo

total (amount) 共计 gòng jì

tough (food) 硬 yìng

tourist 游人 yóu rén

tourist information office 旅 信息办公室 lǚ yóu xìn xī bà gōng shì

tour 游览 yóu lǎn

tow truck 拖车 tuō chē

wel 毛巾 máo jīn

wer 塔 tǎ

wn 镇 zhèn

wn hall 市政厅 shì zhèng tīng

wn map 市区地图 shì qū dì tú

wn square 市中心广场 shì
hōng xīn guǎng chǎng

y 玩具 wán jù

y store 玩具店 wán jù diàn

ck (train) 铁轨 tiě guǐ

ditional 传统 chuán tǒng

ffic light 红绿灯 hóng lǜ
ng

ail 山路小径 shān lù xiǎo jìng

ail map 山路图 shān lù tú

in 火车 huǒ chē

in station 火车站 huǒ chē
hàn

ansfer v (change trains/flights)
转 zhuǎn; ~ v (money) 转账
huǎn zhàng

anslate v 翻译 fān yì

ash 垃圾 lā jī

avel agency 旅行社 lǚ xíng shè

avel sickness 晕动病 yūn dòng
ìng

aveler's check 旅行支票 lǚ
íng zhī piào

aveller's cheque [BE] 旅行支
票 lǚ xíng zhī piào

ee 树 shù

trim (hair cut) 剪 jiǎn

trip 旅程 lǚ chéng

trolley [BE] 电车 diàn chē

trousers [BE] 长裤 cháng kù

T-shirt T恤衫 T xù shān

turn off (lights) 关 guān

turn on (lights) 开 kāi

TV 电视 diàn shì

type v 打字 dǎ zì

tyre [BE] 轮胎 lún tāi

U

United Kingdom (U.K.) 英国
yīng guó

United States (U.S.) 美国 měi guó

ugly 难看 nán kàn

umbrella 伞 sǎn

unattended 无人看管 wú rén
kān guǎn

unconscious 没有知觉 méi yǒu
zhī jué

underground [BE] 地下 dì xià

underground station [BE] 地铁
站 dì tiě zhàn

underpants [BE] 内裤 nèi kù

understand v 理解 lǐ jiě

underwear 内衣 nèi yī

unemployed 失业者 shī yè zhě

university 大学 dà xué

unleaded (gas) 无铅 wú qiān

upper 上部 shàng bù

upset stomach 肠胃不适 cháng wèi bú shì

urgent 迫切 pò qiè

urine 尿 niào

use v 使用 shǐ yòng

username 用户名 yòng hù míng

utensil 器皿 qì mǐn

V

vacancy 有空房 yǒu kōng fáng

vacation 休假 xiū jià

vaccination 接种 jiē zhòng

vacuum cleaner 吸尘器 xī chén qì

vagina 阴道 yīn dào

vaginal infection 阴道传染 yīn dào chuán rǎn

valid 合法 hé fǎ

valley 河谷 hé gǔ

valuable 贵重的 guì zhòng de

value 价值 jià zhí

vegetarian 素食者 sù shí zhě

vehicle registration 车辆注册 chē liàng zhù cè

viewpoint [BE] 观点 guān diǎn

village 村庄 cūn zhuāng

vineyard 葡萄园 pú táo yuán

visa 签证 qiān zhèng

visit v 参观 cān guān

visiting hours 探病时间 tàn bìng shí jiān

visually impaired 弱视者 ruò shì zhě

vitamin 维生素 wéi shēng sù

V-neck V领 V lǐng

volleyball game 排球赛 pái qiú sài

vomit v 呕吐 ǒu tù

W

wait v 等待 děng dài; ~ n 等候时间 děng hòu shí jiān

waiter 服务员 fú wù yuán

waiting room 候诊室 hòu zhěn shì

waitress 女服务员 nǚ fú wù yuán

wake v 醒 xǐng

wake-up call 叫醒服务 jiào xǐng fú wù

walk v 走 zǒu; ~ n 步行 bù xíng

walking route 步行路线 bù xíng lù xiàn

wall clock 挂钟 guà zhōng

wallet 钱包 qián bāo

war memorial 战争纪念馆 zhàn zhēng jì niàn guǎn

warm v (something) 温暖 wēn nuǎn; ~ adj (temperature) 暖和 nuǎn huo

washing machine 洗衣机 xǐ yī jī

watch 手表 shǒu biǎo

ater skis 滑水板 huá shuǐ bǎn

terfall 瀑布 pù bù

eather 天气 tiān qì

ek 星期 xīng qī

ekend 周末 zhōu mò

ekly 每周 měi zhōu

lcome v 欢迎 huān yíng

ll-rested 休息得很好 xiū xī
é hěn hǎo

st 西部 xī bù

at 什么 shén me

eelchair 轮椅 lún yǐ

eelchair ramp 轮椅道 lún
ǐ dào

en 什么时候 shén me shí hòu

ere 哪里 nǎ li

ite 白色 bái sè

o 谁 shuí/shéi

dowed 寡居 guǎ jū

fe 妻子 qī zi

ndow 窗 chuāng

ndow case 橱窗 chú chuāng

ne list 酒类表 jiǔ lèi biǎo

reless internet 无线互联网
ú xiàn hù lián wǎng

reless internet service 无线
互联网服务 wú xiàn hù lián
ǎng fú wù

reless phone 手机 shǒu jī

th 跟 gēn

thdraw v 退出 tuì chū

withdrawal (bank) 取钱 qǔ qián

without 没有 méi yǒu

wok 炒锅 chǎo guō

woman 妇女 fù nǚ

wool 羊毛 yáng máo

work v 工作 gōng zuò

wrap v (a package) 包 bāo

wrist 手腕 shǒu wàn

write v 写 xiě

Y

year 年 nián

yellow 黄色 huáng sè

yes 是 shì

yesterday 昨天 zuó tiān

young 年轻 nián qīng

you're welcome 没关系 méi
guān xi

youth hostel 青年旅舍 qīng nián
lǚ shè

yuan 元 yuán

Z

zoo 动物园 dòng wù yuán

Chinese–English

A

ā sī pǐ lín 阿斯匹林 aspirin
ài 爱 love
ài ěr lán 爱尔兰 Ireland
ài ěr lán rén 爱尔兰人 Irish
ài zī bìng 爱滋病 AIDS
ān jiǎn 安检 security
ān jìng 安静 quiet
ān quán 安全 safe (protected)
àn 按 v push
àn mó 按摩 massage
āng zāng 肮脏 dirty
áng guì 昂贵 expensive
ào dà lì yà rén 澳大利亚人
Australian

B

bā léi 芭蕾 ballet
bá 拔 v extract (tooth)
bái sè 白色 white
bǎi huò shāng diàn 百货商店
department store
bàn 半 half
bàn gōng jīn 半公斤 half-kilo
bàn gōng shì 办公室 office
bàn gōng shí jiān 办公时间
office hours
bàn lǐ dēng jī shǒu xù 办理登机
手续 check-in (airport)

bàn rù zhù 办入住 check-in (h
bàn xiǎo shí 半小时 half hour
bāng zhù 帮助 help
bàng 磅 pound (weight)
bàng qiú 棒球 baseball
bāo 包 v wrap (a package)
bāo guǒ 包裹 package
bāo kuò 包括 v include
bǎo xiān mó 保鲜膜 plastic wr
[cling film BE]
bǎo xiǎn 保险 insurance
bǎo xiǎn gōng sī 保险公司
insurance company
bǎo xiǎn guì 保险柜 safe (thin
bǎo xiǎn kǎ 保险卡 insurance
bǎo cún 保存 v save (on a comp
bǎo mǔ 保姆 babysitter
bào guāng 曝光 exposure (film
bào qiàn 抱歉 sorry
bào tān 报摊 newsstand
bào zhǐ 报纸 newspaper
bēi bāo 背包 backpack
bēi zi 杯子 cup
běi bù 北部 north
bèi bù 背部 back (body part)
bèi qiǎng le 被抢了 robbed
bèi tōu le 被偷了 被偷了 stolen
bēng dài 绷带 bandage
bí zi 鼻子 nose

笔 pen

ji ní yǒng zhuāng 比基尼泳
装 bikini

bǐ jì 笔记 bill [note BE]

sà diàn 比萨店 pizzeria

yùn tào 避孕套 condom

an gēng lù xiàn 变更路线
alternate route

àn mì 便秘 constipated

àn yā qì 变压器 adapter

āo běn 标本 specimen

āo zhì 标志 symbol (keyboard)

āo gé 表格 form (fill-in)

é zhēn 别针 brooch

ng 冰 ice

ng lěng 冰冷 icy

ng qiú 冰球 ice hockey

ng xiāng 冰箱 refrigerator

ng 病 sick [ill BE]

hào 拨号 v dial

li 玻璃 glass (material)

li bēi 玻璃 glass (drinking)

li tiáo liào píng 玻璃调料瓶
carafe

jīn 铂金 platinum

wù guǎn 博物馆 museum

zi 脖子 neck

/ bù 不 no

guì 不贵 inexpensive

xiàn shǐ yòng cì shù de 不限使
用次数的 multiple-trip (ticket)

bǔ yǎng 哺养 v feed

bù fen 部分 portion

bù jiàn 部件 part (for car)

bù luò fēn 布洛芬 ibuprofen

bù xíng 步行 n walk

bù xíng lù xiàn 步行路线 walking
route

C

cā 擦 mop

cài dān 菜单 menu

cān guān 参观 v visit

cān guǎn 餐馆 restaurant

cān jīn 餐巾 napkin

cán jí 残疾 handicapped [disabled
BE]

cán jí rén tōng dào 残疾人通
道 handicapped- [disabled- BE]
accessible

cāng 舱 cabin

cāo chǎng 操场 playground

CD CD CD

cè liáng 测量 v measure (someone)

chā cuò 差错 mistake

chā rù 插入 v insert (on an ATM)

chā zi 叉子 fork

chá chí 茶匙 teaspoon

chá guǎn 茶馆 teahouse

chái yóu 柴油 diesel

cháng 长 long

cháng chang 尝尝 v taste

cháng kù 长裤 pants [trousers BE]

cháng wèi bú shì 肠胃不适 upset stomach

cháng xiù zi 长袖子 long sleeves

cháng zi 肠子 intestine

chāo guò 超过 excess

chāo jí 超级 super (fuel)

chāo jí shì chǎng 超级市场 supermarket

chāo sù kāi chē 超速开车 speeding

chǎo guō 炒锅 wok

chē kù 车库 garage

chē liàng zhù cè 车辆注册 vehicle registration

chén liè chú 陈列橱 display case

chèn shān 衬衫 shirt

chéng bǎo 城堡 castle

chéng kè 乘客 passenger

chī 吃 v eat

chī yào 吃药 v take medicine

chí táng 池塘 pond

chǐ cùn 尺寸 size

chì tǔ táo 赤土陶 terracotta

chōng diàn 充电 v recharge

chōng làng bǎn 冲浪板 surfboard

chōng xuè 充血 congestion

chóng fù 重复 v repeat

chóng yǎo 虫咬 insect bite

chóng zi 虫子 bug

chū gù zhàng 出故障 breakdown

chū kǒu 出口 n exit

chū nà yuán 出纳员 cashier

chū qù 出去 v exit

chū xí 出席 v attend

chū xué zhě 初学者 beginner (level)

chū zū chē 出租车 rental car, ta

chū zū qì chē 出租汽车 car re [hire BE]

chú chuāng 橱窗 window case

chú fáng 厨房 kitchen

chú fáng xī zhǐ 厨房锡纸 aluminum [kitchen BE] foil

chǔ fāng yào 处方药 prescript

chǔ xù 储蓄 savings (account)

chuán rǎn 传染 infected

chuán rǎn de 传染的 contagio

chuán sòng dài 传送带 convey belt

chuán tǒng 传统 traditional

chuán zhēn 传真 n fax

chuán zhēn hào 传真号 fax number

chuāng 窗 window

chuáng 床 bed

chuáng dān 床单 sheet

chuǎng rù 闯入 break-in (burgla

chuī fēng jī 吹风机 hair dryer

chuí zi 锤子 hammer

chún yín 纯银 sterling silver

cí qì 瓷器 china

n zhuāng 村庄 village
n chǔ kǎ 存储卡 memory card
n qián 存钱 v deposit
ò guò 错过 missing

---

chē 搭车 v hitchhike
diàn hào mǎ 电话号码 phone number
bāo 打包 v pack
diàn huà 打电话 v call
huǒ jī 打火机 lighter
kāi 打开 v open
rǎo 打扰 v bother
yìn 打印 v print
zì 打字 v type
大 big
jiào táng 大教堂 cathedral
shà 大厦 building
tuǐ 大腿 thigh
xué 大学 university
i bàn chù 代办处 agency
i lái 带来 v bring
i zǎo cān de lǚ diàn 带早餐的旅店 bed and breakfast
i zi 袋子 bag
n chéng 单程 one-way (ticket)
n dú 单独 alone
n rén chuáng 单人床 single bed
n rén fáng jiān 单人房间 single room

dān shēn 单身 single (unmarried)
dān xíng dào 单行道 one-way street
dāng dì 当地 local
dāo zi 刀子 knife
dǎo máng quǎn 导盲犬 guide dog
dào dá 到达 v arrive
dào kōng 倒空 v empty
dào lù 道路 path
dēng 灯 light (overhead)
dēng jī 登机 v board
dēng jī mén 登机门 gate (airport)
dēng jī pái 登机牌 boarding pass
dēng lù 登录 log on
děng dài 等待 v wait
děng hòu shí jiān 等候时间 n wait
dī 滴 drop (medicine)
dī 低 low
dǐ dá 抵达 arrivals (airport)
dì bǎn 地板 floor
dì tiě 地铁 subway [underground BE]
dì tiě zhàn 地铁站 subway [underground BE] station
dì tú 地图 n map
dì zhǐ 地址 address
dié zi 碟子 dish (kitchen)
diān xián 癫痫 epileptic
diǎn 点 light (cigarette)
diǎn cài 点菜 v order

diǎn xīn diàn 点心店 pastry shop
diàn 垫 sanitary napkin [pad BE]
diàn chā zuò 电插座 electric outlet
diàn chē 电车 trolley
diàn chí 电池 battery
diàn dēng pào 电灯泡 lightbulb
diàn dòng zì xíng chē 电动自行车 moped
diàn fàn guō 电饭锅 rice cooker
diàn huà 电话 telephone, phone call
diàn huà hào mǎ 电话号码 phone
diàn huà kǎ 电话卡 phone card
diàn shàn 电扇 fan (appliance)
diàn shì 电视 TV
diàn tī 电梯 elevator [lift BE]
diàn yǐng 电影 movie
diàn yǐng yuàn 电影院 movie theater
diàn yóu dì zhǐ 电邮地址 e-mail address
diàn zǐ piào 电子票 e-ticket
diàn zǐ yóu jiàn 电子邮件 n e-mail
diāo kè 雕刻 v engrave
diāo xiàng 雕像 statue
diū shī 丢失 v lose (something)
dōng bù 东部 east
dòng 洞 cave
dòng mài 动脉 artery

dòng wù 动物 animal
dòng wù yuán 动物园 zoo
dǒu qiào 陡峭 steep
dòu rén xǐ ài 逗人喜爱 cute
dú yào 毒药 poison
dǔ bó yú lè chǎng 赌博娱乐场 casino
dù 度 degrees (temperature)
duǎn kù 短裤 shorts
duǎn xiǎo 短小 short
duǎn xiù 短袖 short sleeves
duàn 断 v break (tooth)
duàn kāi 断开 disconnect (computer)
duì 队 team
duì fāng fù fèi diàn huà 对方付费电话 v call collect [reverse charges) BE]
duì huàn 兑换 v exchange (money)
duì huàn lǜ 兑换率 exchange r
duì xiàn jīn 兑现金 v cash
dùn 炖 stewed
duō shǎo 多少 how much
duō xuě 多雪 snowy
duō yǔ 多雨 rainy
DVD DVD DVD

E

é wài 额外 extra
ě xin 恶心 nauseous

...kē yī shēng 儿科医生 pediatrician

...tóng cài dān 儿童菜单 children's menu

...tóng fàn liàng 儿童饭量 children's portion

...tóng yóu yǒng chí 儿童游泳也 kiddie [paddling BE] pool

...tóng zuò yǐ 儿童座椅 child's seat

...duo 耳朵 ear

...duo téng 耳朵疼 earache

...huán 耳环 earrings

...jī 耳机 headphones

...chuán zhēn 发传真 v fax

...diàn yóu 发电邮 v e-mail

...duǎn xìn 发短信 v text (send a message)

...huò piào 发货票 invoice

...shāo 发烧 fever

...yīn 发音 v pronounce

...kuǎn 罚款 fine (fee)

...jiāo 发胶 gel (hair)

...láng 珐琅 enamel (jewelry)

...láng 发廊 hair salon

...xíng 发型 hairstyle

...xíng shī 发型师 hairstylist

...n yì 翻译 v translate

...n huán 返还 round-trip [return BE]

fàn 饭 meal

fàn tīng 饭厅 dining room

fāng xiàng 方向 direction

fāng xiāng liáo fǎ 芳香疗法 aromatherapy

fáng huǒ mén 防火门 fire door

fáng jiān 房间 room

fáng jiān yào shi 房间钥匙 room key

fáng shài shuāng 防晒霜 sunblock

fáng zi 房子 house

fēi chǔ fāng yào 非处方药 over the counter [unbranded BE] (medication)

fēi jī 飞机 airplane

fēi jī chǎng 飞机场 airport

féi zào 肥皂 soap

fěi cuì 翡翠 jade

fèi 肺 lung

fèi xū 废墟 ruins

fèi yòng 费用 fee

fēn jī 分机 extension (phone)

fēn jū 分居 separated (marriage)

fēn zhōng 分钟 minute

fěn hóng sè 粉红色 pink

fēng lì 锋利 sharp

fú wù 服务 service (in a restaurant)

fú wù tái 服务台 reservation desk

fú wù yuán 服务员 waiter

fú zhuāng diàn 服装店 clothing store

fǔ shì 俯视 overlook (scenic place)

fù biāo tí 副标题 subtitle

fù chǎn kē yī shī 妇产科医师 gynecologist

fù jiā fèi 附加费 cover charge

fù jìn 附近 near

fù nǚ 妇女 woman

fù qīn 父亲 father

fù xiè 腹泻 diarrhea

fù yìn jiàn 复印件 photocopy

fù zuò yòng 副作用 side effect

G

gǎi 改 v alter (clothing)

gài yìn 盖印 v stamp (a ticket)

gān jìng 干净 adj clean

gān xǐ diàn 干洗店 dry cleaner

gān zàng 肝脏 liver (body part)

gǎn mào 感冒 cold (sickness)

gǎn shí jiān 赶时间 rush

gǎn xiè 感谢 v thank

gāo 高 high

gāo ěr fū qiú bǐ sài 高尔夫球比赛 golf tournament

gāo ěr fū qiú chǎng 高尔夫球场 golf course

gāo jiǎo yǐ 高脚椅 highchair

gāo sù gōng lù 高速公路 highway [motorway BE]

gē bo 胳膊 arm

gē jù 歌剧 opera

gē jù yuàn 歌剧院 opera house

gé yè 隔夜 overnight

gè rén mì mǎ 个人密码 personal identification number (PIN)

gěi 给 v give

gēn 跟 with

gèng dī 更低 lower

gèng duō 更多 more

gèng hǎo 更好 better

gèng kuài 更快 faster

gèng màn 更慢 slower

gèng pián yi 更便宜 cheaper

gèng xiǎo 更小 smaller

gèng zǎo 更早 earlier

gōng diàn 宫殿 palace

gōng gòng 公共 public

gōng gòng qì chē 公共汽车 bus

gōng gòng qì chē piào 公共汽车票 bus ticket

gōng gòng qì chē yóu lǎn 公共汽车游览 bus tour

gōng gòng qì chē zhàn 公共汽车站 bus station, bus stop

gōng jī 攻击 attack (on person)

gōng jīn 公斤 kilo(gram)

gōng lǐ 公里 kilometer

gōng shēng 公升 liter

gōng yòng diàn huà 公用电话

...ay phone

...ng yù 公寓 apartment

...ng yuán 公园 *n* park

...ng zuò 工作 *v* work

...ng láng ér tóng yóu xì chǎng 拱
...郭 儿童游戏场 arcade

...ng jì 共计 total (amount)

...u 够 *v* reach

...u wù 购物 shop

...u wù lán zǐ 购物篮子 basket
(grocery store)

...u wù qū 购物区 shopping area

...u wù zhōng xīn 购物中心
hopping mall [centre BE]

...diǎn yīn yuè 古典音乐
...assical music

...dǒng diàn 古店 antiques store

...tou 骨头 bone

...dìng jià gé cài dān 价格固定
...的菜单 fixed-price menu

...wèn 顾问 consultant

...yòng 雇用 *v* rent [hire BE]

...ǎ jū 寡居 widowed

...à hào xìn 挂号信 registered mail

...à zhōng 挂钟 wall clock

...ǎi jiǎo chù 拐角处 around (the
...orner)

...ān 关 turn off (lights)

...ān bì 关闭 closed

...ān diǎn 观点 overlook [viewpoint
...E]

guān guāng 观光 sightseeing

guān guāng lǚ yóu 观光旅游
sightseeing tour

guān jié 关节 joint (body part)

guān jié yán 关节炎 arthritis

guān mén 关门 *v* close (a shop)

guān shuì 关税 duty (tax)

guān xì 关系 relationship

guàn 罐 pot

guàn zhuāng shí pǐn 罐装食品
canned good

guàn zi 罐子 jar

guī huán 归还 *v* return

guì zhòng de 贵重的 valuable

guó jí 国籍 nationality

guó jì 国际 international (airport
area)

guó jì háng bān 国际航班
international flight

guó jì xué shēng zhèng 国际学
生证 international student card

guó jiā dài hào 国家代号 country
code

guó nèi 国内 domestic

guó nèi háng bān 国内航班
domestic flight

guò dào 过道 aisle

guò mǐn 过敏 allergic

guò mǐn fǎn yìng 过敏反应
allergic reaction

guò shú 过熟 overdone

H

hǎi 海 sea

hǎi guān 海关 customs

hǎi tān 海滩 beach

hái zi 孩子 child

hǎn jiàn 罕见 rare (object)

háng bān 航班 flight

háng kōng gōng sī 航空公司 airline

háng kōng xìn 航空信 airmail

hǎo 好 good, nice, OK

hē 喝 v drink

hé 河 river

hé fǎ 合法 valid

hé gǔ 河谷 valley

hè sè 褐色 brown

hēi àn 黑暗 dark

hēi sè 黑色 black

hóng lǜ dēng 红绿灯 traffic light

hóng sè 红色 red

hóu lóng 喉咙 throat

hóu lóng tòng 喉咙痛 sore throat

hòu jī tīng 候机厅 terminal (airport)

hòu mian 后面 behind (direction)

hòu zhěn shì 候诊室 waiting room

hū xī 呼吸 v breathe

hú 湖 lake

hù fà sù 护发素 conditioner

hù lián wǎng 互联网 internet

hù lián wǎng fú wù 互联网服务 internet service

hù shi 护士 nurse

hù zhào 护照 passport

hù zhào guǎn zhì 护照管制 passport control

huā 花 flower

huā fèi 花费 v cost

huā fěn zhèng 花粉症 hay fever

huá shuǐ bǎn 滑水板 water ski

huá tǐng 划艇 rowboat

huá xuě 滑雪 ski

huá xuě bǎn 滑雪板 snowboard

huá xuě gǎn 滑雪杆 poles (ski)

huá xuě lǎn chē 滑雪缆车 ski

huà zhuāng rǔ yè 化妆乳液 lotion

huái yùn 怀孕 pregnant

huài le 坏了 damaged

huān yíng 欢迎 v welcome

huàn chē 换车 v change (buses)

huàn dì fang 换地方 n exchange (place)

huàn niào bù 换尿布 n change (baby)

huàn qián 换钱 v change (money)

huáng sè 黄色 yellow

huī sè 灰色 gray

huí shōu 回收 recycling

huì yì 会议 conference, meeting

huì yì shì 会议室 meeting room

yì tīng 会议厅 convention hall

yuán zhèng 会员证 membership card

ǒ 火 fire

ǒ chái 火柴 *n* match (sports)

ǒ chē zhàn 火车站 train [railway BE] station

ǒ chē 火车 train

ò bì 货币 currency

ò bì duì huàn 货币兑换 currency exchange

ò bì duì huàn jú 货币兑换局 currency exchange office

---

jī è 饥饿 hungry

ǒu 肌肉 muscle

huī 脊椎 spine (body part)

ōng 技工 mechanic

huà shēng yù yào piàn 计划生育药片 Pill (birth control)

iàn guǎn 纪念馆 memorial (place)

iàn pǐn 纪念品 souvenir

iàn pǐn shāng diàn 纪念品商店 souvenir store

hí qì 计时器 meter (parking)

hí xùn xī 即时讯息 instant message

uàn jī 计算机 computer

dà hào 加大号 plus size

jià gé 价格 price

jiá kè 夹克 jacket

jiā ná dà 加拿大 Canada

jiā ná dà rén 加拿大人 Canadian

jiā rè 加热 heat

jiā rè qì 加热器 heater

jià rì 假日 vacation [holiday BE]

jiā rù 加入 *v* join

jiā tíng 家庭 family

jiā yòng wù pǐn 家用物品 household good

jiā yóu zhàn 加油站 gas [petrol BE] station

jiǎ yá 假牙 denture

jià zhí 价值 value

jiān bǎng 肩膀 shoulder

jiān dū 监督 supervision

jiān guō 煎锅 frying pan

jiān zhí 兼职 part-time

jiǎn 剪 *v* cut (hair)

jiǎn chá 检查 *v* check (something)

jiǎn dāo 剪刀 scissors

jiàn 件 case (amount)

jiàn kāng 健康 health

jiàn kāng shí pǐn shāng diàn 健康食品商店 health food store

jiàn miàn 见面 *v* meet (someone)

jiǎng huà 讲话 *v* speak

jiāo huàn 交换 *v* exchange (goods)

jiāo juǎn 胶卷 film (camera)

jiāo xiǎo 娇小 petite

jiǎo 脚 foot
jiǎo wàn 脚腕 ankle
jiǎo zhǐ 脚趾 toe
jiào shǎo 较少 less
jiào táng 教堂 church
jiào xǐng fú wù 叫醒服务 wake-up call
jiē shòu 接受 v receive
jiē zhòng 接种 vaccination
jié hūn 结婚 v marry
jié shù 结束 v end
jiě mèi 姐妹 sister
jiè jì kǎ 借记卡 debit card
jiè shào 介绍 v introduce
jiè zhi 戒指 ring
jīn tiān 今天 today
jīn wǎn 今晚 tonight
jīn zi 金子 gold
jǐn jí chū kǒu 紧急出口 emergency exit
jǐn jí zhuàng tài 紧急状态 emergency
jìn 近 close
jìn rù 进入 v enter, access
jìn yān 禁烟 non-smoking
jìn zhǐ 禁止 v prohibit
jīng jì cāng 经济舱 economy class
jīng lǐ 理 manager
jīng qī fù tòng 经期腹痛 menstrual cramp
jǐng chá 警察 police

jǐng chá jú 警察局 police static
jǐng chá bào gào 警察报告 p report
jǐng tài lán 景泰蓝 cloisonné
jìng piàn 镜片 lens
jiǔ bā 酒吧 bar (place)
jiǔ diàn 酒店 liquor store [off-licence BE]
jiù hù chē 救护车 ambulance
jiǔ lèi biǎo 酒类表 wine list
jiù shēng yī 救生衣 life jacket
jiù shēng yuán 救生员 lifegua
jū zhù 居住 v live
jú sè 桔色 orange (color)
jù jué 拒绝 v decline (credit carc
jù lè bù 俱乐部 club
jù yuàn 剧院 theater
jué shì yuè 爵士乐 jazz
jué shì yuè jù lè bù 爵士乐俱 部 jazz club

K

kā fēi diàn 咖啡店 coffee shop
kǎ 卡 card
kǎ lù lǐ 卡路里 calorie
kāi 开 turn on (lights)
kāi chē 开车 v drive
kāi chǔ fāng 开处方 v prescrib
kāi fù kuǎn dān 开付款单 v ▶ (charge)
kāi guàn qì 开罐器 can opene

sāi zuàn 开塞钻 corkscrew

shǐ 开始 v begin

shǐ 开始 v start

wèi cài 开胃菜 appetizer [starter BE]

zhe 开着 adj open

kàn 看 v look

n jiàn 看见 v see

ng shēng sù 抗生素 antibiotic

o ròu 烤肉 barbecue

o guò dào de wèi zi 靠过道的
位子 aisle seat

lóng xiāng shuǐ 科隆香水
cologne

xué 科学 science

sou 咳嗽 cough

kǒu 可口 delicious

pà 可怕 terrible

渴 thirsty

克 gram

cāng 客舱 cabin

chéng 课程 lesson

fáng qīng jié fú wù 客房清洁
服务 housekeeping services

fáng sòng cān fú wù 客房送
餐服务 room service

ng tiáo 空调 air conditioning

u dài 口袋 pocket

u xiāng táng 口香糖 chewing
um

u yì yuán 口译员 interpreter

kù wà 裤袜 pantyhose [tights BE]

kuài 快 express

kuài cān 快餐 fast food

kuài sù 快速 fast

kuài zi 筷子 chopsticks

kùn nan 困难 difficult

L

lā v pull

lā jī 垃圾 trash [rubbish BE]

lā jī dài 垃圾袋 garbage [rubbish BE] bag

là 辣 hot (spicy)

lái 来 v come

lán sè 蓝色 blue

lán qiú 篮球 basketball

lǎn chē 缆车 cable car

lǎn chē piào 缆车票 lift pass

làng màn 浪漫 romantic

lǎo 老 old

lǎo nián rén 老年人 senior citizen

lè qù 乐趣 pleasure

léi yǔ 雷雨 thunderstorm

lèi gǔ 肋骨 rib (body part)

lèi le 累了 tired

lěng 冷 cold (temperature)

lěng dòng jī 冷冻机 freezer

lí hūn 离婚 v divorce

lí kāi 离开 departures

lí mǐ 厘米 centimeter

lǐ bài 礼拜 mass (church service)

lǐ chéng shù 里程数 mileage
lǐ fà 理发 haircut
lǐ fà shī 理发师 barber
lǐ jiě 理解 v understand
lǐ pǐn diàn 礼品店 gift shop
lǐ wù 礼物 gift
lián jiē 连接 v connect (internet)
lián xì 联系 v contact
lián yī qún 连衣裙 dress (piece of clothing)
liáng 凉 cool (temperature)
liáng bēi 量 measuring cup
liáng chí 量匙 measuring spoon
liáng xié 凉鞋 sandals
lín shí 临时 temporary
lín yù 淋浴 shower
líng qián 零钱 v change (money)
lǐng dài 领带 tie (clothing)
lǐng shì guǎn 领事馆 consulate
lìng rén jīng qí de 令人惊奇的 amazing
liú dòng xìng 流动性 mobility
liú xíng yīn yuè 流行音乐 pop music
liú xuè 流血 v bleed
lóng 聋 deaf
lóu céng 楼层 floor [storey BE]
lú zi 炉子 stove
lù quán 路权 right of way
lù xiàn 路线 route
lù xiàn tú 路线图 road map

lù yíng 露营 v camp
lù yíng dì 露营地 campsite
lù yíng lú 露营炉 camping stove
lún dù 轮渡 ferry
lún tāi 轮胎 tire [tyre BE]
lún yǐ 轮椅 wheelchair
lún yǐ dào 轮椅道 wheelchair ramp
lǚ chéng 旅程 trip
lǚ guǎn 旅馆 hotel
lǚ xíng shè 旅行社 travel agen
lǚ xíng zhī piào 旅行支票 travelers check [cheque BE]
lǚ yóu xìn xī bàn gōng shì 旅游 信息办公室 tourist informa office
lǚ shè 旅舍 hostel
lǜ sè 绿色 green
lǜ shī 律师 lawyer

M

má zuì 麻醉 anesthesia
mǎi 买 v buy
mài 卖 v sell
mài huā rén 卖花人 florist
màn màn de 慢慢地 slowly
máng cháng 盲肠 appendix (b part)
máo jīn 毛巾 towel
máo yī 毛衣 sweater
mào zi 帽子 hat

éi guān xi 没关系 you're welcome

éi shén me 没什么 nothing

éi yǒu 没有 without

éi yǒu zhī jué 没有知觉 unconscious

ěi 每 every

ěi tiān 每天 per day

ěi wǎn 每晚 per night

ěi xiǎo shí 每小时 per hour

ěi xīng qī 每星期 per week

ěi zhōu 每周 weekly

ěi guó 美国 United States (U.S.)

ěi guó rén 美国人 American

ěi jiǎ shā lóng 美甲沙龙 nail salon

ěi lì 美丽 beautiful

ěi yuán 美元 dollar (U.S.)

ǐ huáng sè 米黄色 beige

ì mǎ 密码 password

án hua 棉花 cotton

ǎn fèi 免费 free

ǎn shuì 免税 duty-free

àn bāo diàn 面包店 bakery

àn bù 面部 facial

àn jīn zhǐ 面巾纸 tissue

àn kǒng 面孔 face

ín jiān yīn yuè 民间音乐 folk music

íng piàn 名片 business card

íng tiān 明天 tomorrow

míng xìn piàn 明信片 postcard

míng zì 名字 name

mó sī 摩丝 mousse (hair)

mó tuō chē 摩托车 motorcycle

mǔ qīn 母亲 mother

mǔ rǔ wèi yǎng 母乳喂养 breastfeed

mù tàn 木炭 charcoal

N

ná zǒu 拿走 to go [take away BE]

nǎ lǐ 哪里 where

nà 那 that

nà lǐ 那里 there

nǎi fěn 奶粉 formula (baby)

nǎi píng 奶瓶 baby bottle

nán 南 south

nán hái 男孩 boy

nán kàn 难看 ugly

nán nèi kù 男内裤 briefs (clothing)

nán péng you 男朋友 boyfriend

nán rén 男人 man

nán tóng xìng liàn 男同性恋 gay

nán tóng xìng liàn jiǔ bā 男同性恋酒吧 gay bar

nán tóng xìng liàn jù lè bù 男同性恋俱乐部 gay club

nèi kù 内裤 underwear [underpants BE]

nǐ hǎo 你好 hello

nián 年 year

nián líng 年龄 age
nián qīng 年轻 young
niǎo 鸟 bird
niào 尿 urine
niào bù 尿布 diaper [nappy BE]
niú zǎi kù 牛仔裤 jeans
niǔ shāng 扭伤 sprain
nóng chǎn pǐn 农产品 produce
nóng chǎn pǐn shāng diàn 农产品商店 produce store
nóng chǎng 农场 farm
nuǎn huo 暖和 *adj* warm (temperature)
nuǎn qì 暖气 heat [heating BE]
nǚ chèn shān 女衬衫 blouse
nǚ fú wù yuán 女服务员 waitress
nǚ hái 女孩 girl
nǚ péng you 女朋友 girlfriend

O

ǒu tù 呕吐 *v* vomit

P

pái qiú sài 排球赛 volleyball game
pán zi 盘子 plate
páng guāng 膀胱 bladder
pǎo mǎ chǎng 跑马场 racetrack
pèi cài 配菜 side dish
pèi yào fāng 配药方 *v* fill [make up BE] (a prescription)
pēn fà jì 喷发剂 hairspray

pēn quán 喷泉 fountain
pēng tiáo 烹调 *v* cook
pēng tiáo méi qì 烹调煤气 cooking gas
péng you 朋友 friend
pí dài 皮带 belt
pí fū 皮肤 skin
pí gé 皮革 leather
pí zhěn 皮疹 rash
pì gu 屁股 buttocks
pián yi 便宜 cheap
piàn 片 piece
piàn jì 片剂 tablet (medicine)
piào 票 ticket
pīn xiě 拼写 *v* spell
pín xuè 贫血 anemic
píng 瓶 bottle
píng dǐ guō 平底锅 saucepan
píng qǐ zi 瓶启子 bottle opener
pò le 破了 broken
pò qiè 迫切 urgent
pú táo yuán 葡萄园 vineyard
pǔ tóng 普通 regular
pù bù 瀑布 waterfall
pù wèi 铺位 berth

Q

qī zi 妻子 wife
qī jiān 期间 period (of time)
qī qi 漆器 lacquerware
qí guài 奇怪 strange

fēi 起飞 v leave

tǒng 气筒 air pump

chuǎn 气喘 asthmatic

chē 汽车 car

chē zhàn 汽车站 bus station

chē zuò wèi 汽车座位 car seat

chuán 汽船 motor boat

yóu 汽油 gas [petrol BE]

mǐn 器皿 utensil

ān yǐn lǎn chē 牵引缆车 drag lift

ān zhèng 签证 visa

ān zì 签字 v sign

ān qián 钱 money

ān bāo 钱包 purse, wallet

án shuǐ 潜水 v dive

án shuǐ yòng jù 潜水用具 diving equipment

īng jiān 强奸 rape

ǎng 抢 v mug

ǎng duó 抢夺 v rob

áo liáng 桥梁 bridge

ào bì 峭壁 cliff

ē piàn 切片 slice (of something)

ņ wěn 亲吻 v kiss

ng biàn xiǎo chuáng 轻便小床 cot

ng biàn zhé dié tǎng yǐ 轻便折叠躺椅 deck chair

ng chú 清除 v clear (on an ATM)

qīng jié chǎn pǐn 清洁产品 cleaning product

qīng jié chǎn pǐn gōng yìng 清洁产品供应 cleaning supplies

qīng méi sù 青霉素 penicillin

qīng nián lǚ shè 青年旅舍 youth hostel

qīng xǐ 清洗 v clean

qīng zhēn shí pǐn 清真食品 halal

qīng zhēn sì 清真寺 mosque

qíng lǎng 晴朗 sunny

qǐng 请 please

qiú pāi 球拍 racket (sports)

qū gùn qiú 曲棍球 hockey

qū hà 区号 area code

qū yù 区域 region

qǔ 取 pick up (something)

qǔ qián 取钱 withdrawal (bank)

qǔ xiāo 取消 v cancel

qù 去 v go (somewhere)

quán miàn fú wù 全面服务 full service

quán jī bǐ sài 击比赛 boxing match

qún zi 裙子 skirt

R

rè 热 hot (temperature)

rè shuǐ 热水 hot water

rén mín bì 人民币 Ren Min Bi

rén mín dà huì táng 人民大会堂 Great Hall of the People

rèn hé dōng xī 任何东西 anything

rì běn 日本 Japanese (restaurant)

rì chéng biǎo 日程表 *n* schedule

rì qī 日期 date (calendar)

róng yì 容易 easy

rǔ fáng 乳房 breast

rǔ táng guò mǐn 乳糖过敏 lactose intolerant

rù chǎng 入场 admission

rù kǒu 入口 entrance

ruò shì zhě 弱视者 visually impaired

S

sǎn 伞 umbrella

sǎo miáo qì 扫描器 scanner

sēn lín 森林 forest

shā chóng jì 杀虫剂 insect repellent

shā guō 砂锅 clay pot

shā mò 沙漠 desert

shài shāng 晒伤 sunburn

shān 山 mountain

shān dì chē 山地车 mountain bike

shān dǐng 山顶 peak (of a mountain)

shān lù tú 山路图 trail map

shān lù xiǎo jìng 山路小径 trail

shān chú 删除 *v* delete

shāng kǒu 伤口 *n* cut (injury)

shāng xīn 伤心 sad

shāng diàn mù lù 商店目录 s directory

shāng wù 商务 business

shāng wù cāng 商务舱 busine class

shāng yè zhōng xīn 商业中心 business center

shàng bù 上部 upper

shàng wǔ 上午 a.m.

shāo 烧 *v* burn

sháo zǐ 勺子 spoon

shǎo xǔ 少许 little

shé tóu 舌头 tongue

shè bèi 设备 equipment

shè shì 摄氏 Celsius

shè yǐng 摄影 photography

shēn bào 申报 *v* declare

shēn shēn de 深深地 deeply

shén me 什么 what

shén me shí hòu 什么时候 when

shèn zàng 肾脏 kidney (body p

shēng jiàng yǐ 升降椅 chair lif

shēng rì 生日 birthday

shī mián 失眠 insomnia

shī qù 失去 lost

shī wù zhāo lǐng chù 失物招 处 lost and found

shī yè zhě 失业者 unemployed

shí èr 十二 dozen

í zì lù kǒu 十字路口 intersection

í jiān 时间 time

í jiān biǎo 时间表 schedule [timetable BE]

í wù 食物 food

ǐ yòng 使用 v use

ì chǎng 市场 market

ì qū dì tú 市区地图 town map

ì zhèng tīng 市政厅 town hall

ì zhōng xīn 市中心 downtown

ì zhōng xīn guǎng chǎng 市中心广场 town square

ì hé 适合 fit (clothing)

ì gù 事故 accident

ì yī jiān 试衣间 fitting room

ì 是 yes

ì 是 v be

ì nèi yóu yǒng chí 室内游泳池 indoor pool

ì wài yóu yǒng chí 室外游泳池 outdoor pool

ōu fèi 收费 n charge (cost)

ōu jù 收据 receipt

ǒu 手 hand

ǒu biǎo 手表 watch

ǒu diàn 手电 flashlight

ǒu dòng qì chē 手动汽车 manual car

ǒu jī 手机 cell [mobile BE] phone

ǒu tí xiāng 手提箱 suitcase

shǒu tí xíng li 手提行李 carry-on [hand luggage BE]

shǒu tuī chē 手推车 cart (grocery store)

shǒu wàn 手腕 wrist

shǒu zhǐ 手指 finger

shǒu zhuó 手镯 bracelet

shǒu shì 首饰 jewelry

shòu piào chù 售票处 ticket office

shū 书 book

shū diàn 书店 bookstore

shū fǎ yòng pǐn 书法用品 calligraphy supplies

shū zi 梳子 comb, hairbrush

shú shí 熟食 delicatessen

shù 树 tree

shù mǎ 数码 digital

shù mǎ xiàng jī 数码相机 digital camera

shù mǎ xiàng piàn 数码相片 digital photos

shù mǎ yìn shuā pǐn 数码印刷品 digital prints

shù zì 数字 number

shuāng chéng 双程 round-trip

shuāng rén chuáng 双人床 double bed

shuí/shéi 谁 who

shuǐ cáo 水槽 sink

shuǐ chí 水池 pool

shuǐ jīng 水晶 crystal

shuǐ xià hū xī shè bèi 水下呼吸设备 snorkeling equipment
shuì dài 睡袋 sleeping bag
shuì jiào 睡觉 *v* sleep
shuì yī 睡衣 pajamas
shuì yì 睡意 drowsiness
shuō chàng yuè 说唱乐 rap (music)
sī chóu 丝绸 silk
sī jī jià zhào hào 司机驾照号 driver's license number
sì miào 寺庙 shrine, temple (religious)
sòng 送 *v* send
sù liào bāo zhuāng 塑料包装 plastic wrap [cling film BE]
sù shè 宿舍 dormitory
sù shí zhě 素食者 vegetarian
sù zuì 宿醉 hangover
sūn zi 孙子 grandchild
sǔn shāng 损伤 *v* damage
suǒ 锁 *n* lock

T

T xù shān T恤衫 T-shirt
tǎ 塔 tower
tái jiē 台阶 stairs
tài 太 too
tài yáng 太阳 sun
tài yáng jìng 太阳镜 sunglasses
tài nuò 泰诺 acetaminophen

[paracetamol BE]
tǎn zi 毯子 blanket
tàn bìng shí jiān 探病时间 visiting hours
tāng sháo 汤勺 ceramic spoon
táng guǒ 糖果 candy
táng niào bìng 糖尿病 diabeti
táo qì 陶器 pottery
tè dà hào 特大号 extra large
téng 疼 hurt, pain
tí bāo 提包 purse [handbag BE]
tǐ cāo 体操 gym
tǐ yù 体育 sports
tǐ yù àn mó 体育按摩 sports massage
tǐ yù chǎng 体育场 stadium
tǐ yù yòng pǐn shāng diàn 体育品商店 sporting goods store
tì xū dāo 剃须刀 razor blade
tì xū gāo 剃须膏 shaving cream
tiān 天 day
tiān qì 天气 weather
tián 甜 sweet (taste)
tián diǎn 甜点 candy [sweets BE]
tián chōng wù 填充物 filling (tooth)
tián xiě 填写 fill out (form)
tiáo 条 carton
tiáo zhou 笤帚 broom
tiào wǔ 跳舞 *v* dance
tiě guǐ 铁轨 track (train)

g lì zhàng ài 听力障碍 hearing
 mpaired

g chē 停车 v park

g chē chǎng 停车场 parking lot
 car park BE]

g chē jì shí qì 停车计时器
 arking meter

ng zhī 通知 v notify

ng 铜 copper

ng shì 同事 colleague

ng 痛 pain

u 偷 v steal

u qiè 偷窃 theft

u 头 head (body part)

u děng cāng 头等舱 first class

u fà 头发 hair

u hūn yǎn huā 头昏眼花 dizzy

u kuī 头盔 helmet

u téng 头疼 headache

hù 屠户 butcher

shū guǎn 图书馆 library

 jiàn 推荐 v recommend; ~ n
 ecommendation

 腿 leg

 chū 退出 log off, withdraw

 fáng 退房 check-out (hotel)

 xiū 退休 retired

n xià 吞下 v swallow

ō chē 拖车 tow truck

ō xié 拖鞋 slippers

ō yùn 托运 v check (luggage)

V

V lǐng V领 V-neck

W

wà zi 袜子 sock

wài miàn 外面 outside

wài tào 外套 coat

wán 玩 v play

wán jù 玩具 toy

wán jù diàn 玩具店 toy store

wán jù wá wá 玩具娃娃 doll

wǎn 碗 bowl

wǎn cān 晚餐 dinner

wǎn diǎn 晚点 v delay

wǎn le 晚了 late (time)

wǎn shang 晚上 evening

wǎn shang hǎo 晚上好 good
  evening

wǎng bā 网吧 internet cafe

wǎng qiú 网球 tennis

wēi bō lú 微波炉 microwave

wēi xiǎn 危险 dangerous

wéi 为 for

wéi jīn 围巾 scarf

wéi shēng sù 维生素 vitamin

wèi shēng zhǐ 卫生纸 toilet paper

wèi 喂 v feed

wèi 胃 stomach

wèi téng 胃疼 stomachache

wēn nuǎn 温暖 v warm
  (something)

wēn quán 温泉 hot spring, spa

wén zì 文字 n text (message)

wèn tí 问题 problem, question

wèn xùn chù 问讯处 information desk

wò pù chē 卧铺车 sleeper car

wú jiǔ jīng 无酒精 non-alcoholic

wú liáo de 无聊的 boring

wú qiān 无铅 unleaded (gas)

wú rén kān guǎn 无人看管 unattended

wú wèi 无味 bland

wú xiàn hù lián wǎng 无线互联网 wireless internet

wú xiàn hù lián wǎng fú wù 无线互联网服务 wireless internet service

wú zhī fáng 无脂肪 fat free

wǔ cān 午餐 lunch

wǔ dǎo jù lè bù 舞蹈俱乐部 dance club

wǔ jiān 午间 noon [midday BE]

wǔ yè 午夜 midnight

wù pǐn 物品 goods

X

xī bù 西部 west

xī chén qì 吸尘器 vacuum cleaner

xī fú tào zhuāng 西服套装 suit

xī zhǐ 锡纸 aluminum [kitchen BE] foil

xī gài 膝盖 knee

xī yān 吸烟 v smoke

xī yān qū 吸烟区 smoking (are

xǐ dí jì 洗涤剂 detergent

xǐ huan 喜欢 v like

xǐ shǒu jiān 洗手间 restroom [toilet BE]

xǐ wǎn jī 洗碗机 dishwasher

xǐ wǎn yè 洗碗液 dishwashing liquid

xǐ yī diàn 洗衣店 laundromat [launderette BE]

xǐ yī diàn shè shī 洗衣店设施 laundry facility

xǐ yī fú wù 洗衣服务 laundry service

xǐ yī jī 洗衣机 washing machin

xì jù 戏剧 n play (theatre)

xiá gǔ 峡谷 canyon

xiá gǔ 峡谷 ravine

xià 下 v place (a bet)

xià chē 下车 get off (a train/bus subway)

xià hé 下颌 jaw

xià shuǐ dào shū tōng qì 下水道疏通器 plunger

xià wǔ 下午 afternoon

xià wǔ 下午 p.m.

xià wǔ hǎo 下午好 good after

xià yí gè 下一个 next

xiàn 线 line (train)

 àn chǎng yīn yuè 现场音乐 live music

àn shì 显示 display

àn shì 显示 *v* show

àn jīn 现金 *n* cash

àn zài 现在 now

āng bō 香波 shampoo

àng fǎn 相反 opposite

āng shuǐ 香水 perfume

āng yān 香烟 cigarette

āng zi 箱子 box

àng yòng 享用 *v* enjoy

àng liàn 项链 necklace

àng pí nǎi zuǐ 橡皮奶嘴 pacifier [soother BE]

àng piàn 相片 photo

āo dú yào gāo 消毒药膏 antiseptic cream

āo fáng duì 消防队 fire department

āo shòu shuì 销售税 sales tax

āo 小 small

āo cān guǎn 小餐馆 cafe

āo chǎn zi 小铲子 spatula

āo chī diàn 小吃店 snack bar

āo chuán 小船 boat

āo dào 小道 trail [piste BE]

āo dào lù xiàn tú 小道路线图 trail [piste BE] map

āo jiǔ bā 小酒吧 mini-bar

āo shān 小山 hill

xiǎo shí 小时 hour

xiǎo tōu 小偷 thief

xiǎo xī 小溪 stream

xiǎo xíng kè chē 小型客车 station wagon

xiǎo zǔ 小组 group

xié dài 鞋带 lace

xié diàn 鞋店 shoe store

xié zi 鞋子 shoes

xié wén cū mián bù 斜纹粗棉布 denim

xiě 写 *v* write

xiè xiè 谢谢 thank you

xīn zàng 心脏 heart

xīn zàng bìng 心脏病 heart condition

xīn shǒu 新手 novice (skill level)

xīn xiān 新鲜 fresh

xìn fēng 信封 envelope

xìn jiàn 信件 letter

xìn xī 信息 information (phone); ~ 信息 message

xìn yòng kǎ 信用卡 credit card

xīng qī 星期 week

xíng rén 行人 pedestrian

xíng li 行李 luggage [baggage BE]

xíng li piào 行李票 luggage ticket

xíng li rèn lǐng 行李认领 baggage claim

xíng li tuī chē 行李推车 cart (luggage)

xíng li zàn cún xiāng 行李暂存箱 luggage locker

xǐng 醒 v wake

xìng chuán bō jí bìng 性传播疾病 sexually transmitted disease (STD)

xiōng dì 兄弟 brother

xiōng kǒu 胸口 chest (body part)

xiōng kǒu tòng 胸口痛 chest pain

xiōng zhào 胸罩 bra

xiū dào yuàn 修道院 abbey, monastery

xiū jià 休假 vacation

xiū jiǎo zhǐ jia 修脚趾甲 pedicure

xiū lǐ 修理 v fix (repair), mend

xiū shǒu zhǐ jia 修手指甲 manicure

xū hòu shuǐ 须后水 aftershave

xū yào 需要 v need

xuē zi 靴子 boots

xué shēng 学生 student

xué xí 学习 study

xué xiào 学校 school

xuě jiā 雪茄 cigar

xuě xuē 雪靴 snowshoe

xuè yā 血压 blood pressure

xuè yè 血液 blood

xún huán 环 cycling

Y

yá 牙 tooth

yá gāo 牙膏 toothpaste

yá yī 牙医 dentist

yà má bù 亚麻布 linen

yà zhōu 亚洲 Asian (restaurant)

yān cǎo líng shòu shāng 烟草售商 tobacconist

yán sè 颜色 color

yán sù 严肃 serious

yán tǎo huì 研讨会 seminar

yǎn jīng 眼睛 eye

yǎn jìng 眼镜 glasses

yàn guāng shī 验光师 optician

yáng máo 羊毛 wool

yǎng qì zhì liáo 氧气治疗 oxygen treatment

yáo lán 摇篮 crib

yào 药 medication

yào fáng 药房 pharmacy [chemist BE]

yào gāo 药膏 cream (ointment)

yào sài 要塞 fort

yào shi 钥匙 key

yào shi kǎ 钥匙卡 key card

yào shi quān 钥匙圈 key ring

yào xǐ de yī wù 要洗的衣物 laundry

yě cān qū 野餐区 picnic area

yè 夜 night

yè zǒng huì 夜总会 nightclub

óu 一楼 ground floor
wù 衣物 clothing
wù guì 衣物柜 locker
hēng 医生 doctor
ào 医药 medicine
uàn 医院 hospital
ì 一次 once
ì xìng 一次性 disposable
ì xìng tì dāo 一次性剃刀 disposable razor
ǎo sù 胰岛素 insulin
òng diàn huà 移动电话 cell mobile BE] phone
òu 以后 after, later
ián 以前 before
ǐ 椅子 chair
hù 艺术 arts
iān 一天 one day
iē 一些 some
yuè 音乐 music
yuè huì 音乐会 concert
yuè shāng diàn 音乐商店 music store
yuè tīng 音乐厅 concert hall
dào 阴道 vagina
dào chuán rǎn 阴道传染 vaginal infection
jīng 阴茎 penis
银 silver
háng 银行 bank
liào 饮料 *n* drink

yǐn liào dān 饮料单 drink menu
yǐn yòng shuǐ 饮用水 drinking water
yǐn xíng yǎn jìng 隐形眼镜 contact lens
yǐn xíng yǎn jìng yè 隐形眼镜液 contact lens solution
yīng bàng 英镑 pounds (British sterling)
yīng guó 英国 United Kingdom (U.K.)
yīng guó rén 英国人 British
yīng yǔ 英语 English
yīng ér 婴儿 baby
yīng ér chē 婴儿车 stroller [pushchair BE]
yīng ér zhǐ jīn 婴儿纸巾 baby wipe
yíng yè shí jiān 营业时间 business hours
yìng bì 硬币 coin
yōng bào 拥抱 *v* hug
yòng hù míng 用户名 username
yòng jìn 用尽 exhausted
yòng xìn yòng kǎ fù kuǎn 用信用卡付款 *v* charge (credit card)
yóu 油 oil
yóu jì 邮寄 *v* mail
yóu jiàn 邮件 *n* mail [post BE]
yóu jú 邮局 post office
yóu piào 邮票 *n* stamp (postage)

yóu xiāng 邮箱 mailbox [postbox BE]

yóu tài jiào táng 犹太教堂 synagogue

yóu tài shí pǐn 犹太食品 kosher

yóu dàng zhě 游荡者 loafers

yóu lǎn 游览 excursion, tour

yóu lǎn shèng dì 游览胜地 attraction (place)

yóu lè yuán 游乐园 amusement park

yóu rén 游人 tourist

yóu xì 游戏 game

yóu xì wéi lán 游戏围栏 playpen

yóu yǒng 游泳 v swim

yóu yǒng yī 游泳衣 swimsuit

yǒu kōng fáng 有空房 vacancy

yǒu 有 have

yǒu qù 有趣 interesting

yǒu xī yǐn lì de 有吸引力的 attractive

yú kuài 愉快 happy

yú lè 娱乐 entertainment

yǔ 雨 n rain

yǔ lín 雨林 rainforest

yǔ yī 雨衣 raincoat

yù bào 预报 forecast

yù dìng 预定 v reserve ; ~ n reservation

yù dìng rì chéng 预定日程 v schedule

yù zhī xiàn jīn 预支现金 cash

yù shì 浴室 bathroom [toilet BE]

yuán 元 yuan (currency)

yuán liàng 谅 v excuse

yuán lǐng 圆领 crew neck

yuǎn 远 far

yuàn yán 怨言 complaint

yuē huì 约会 appointment

yuè 月 month

yuè jīng 月经 period (menstrua

yuè jīng shuān 月经栓 tampo

yuè duì 乐队 orchestra

yūn dòng bìng 晕动病 motio sickness

yūn dòng bìng 晕动病 travel sickness

yǔn xǔ 允许 v allow, permit

yùn dòng chǎng 运动场 field (sports)

yùn dòng shān 运动衫 sweat

yùn dòng xié 运动鞋 sneaker

yùn sòng 运送 v ship (mail)

yùn 熨 v press (clothing)

yùn dǒu 熨斗 n iron

yùn yī fu 熨衣服 v iron

Z

zá huò diàn 杂货店 grocery st

zá zhì 杂志 magazine

zài 在 in; on; at

guǎi jiǎo chù 在拐角处 on the corner

jiàn 再见 goodbye

zǎo 早 early

zǎo cān 早餐 breakfast

zǎo chén 早晨 morning

zǎo chen hǎo 早晨好 good morning

zěn me 怎么 how

zhá 闸 brakes (car)

zhàn 站 station, stop

zhàn chǎng 战场 battleground

zhàn tái 站台 platform

zhàn zhēng jì niàn guǎn 战争纪念馆 war memorial

zhàng fu 丈夫 husband

zhàng dān 账单 *n* bill (of sale)

zhàng hù 账户 *n* account

zhàng péng 帐篷 tent

zhàng péng gǎn 帐篷杆 tent pole

zhàng péng zhuāng 帐蓬桩 tent peg

zhāo dài huì 招待会 reception

zhào xiàng jī 照相机 camera

zhào xiàng jī tào 照相机套 camera case

zhào xiàng qì cái shāng diàn 照相器材商店 camera store

zhē 蜇 *v* sting

zhé kòu 折扣 discount

zhè 这 this

zhè lǐ 这里 here

zhēn jiǔ 针灸 acupuncture

zhēn zhū 珍珠 pearl

zhēn zhèng 真正 real

zhěn tóu 枕头 pillow

zhèn 镇 town

zhèn jīng 震惊 stunning

zhēng guō 蒸锅 steamer

zhēng qì yù 蒸汽浴 sauna

zhèng jiàn 证件 identification

zhèng míng 证明 certificate

zhèng shí 证实 *v* confirm

zhèng zhuàng 症状 condition (medical)

zhī fù 支付 *v* pay

zhī piào 支票 *n* check [cheque BE] (payment)

zhī piào zhàng hù 支票账户 checking [current BE] account

zhí 直 straight

zhí wù yuán 植物园 botanical garden

zhǐ hàn lù 止汗露 deodorant

zhǐ 只 only

zhǐ 纸 paper

zhǐ bì 纸币 *n* bill [note BE] (money)

zhǐ jīn 纸巾 paper towel

zhǐ jia 指甲 fingernail

zhǐ jia cuò 指甲锉 nail file

zhǐ nán 指南 *n* guide

zhǐ nán shū 指南书 guide book
zhǐ jiǎ 趾甲 toenail
zhì liàng 质量 quality
zhōng děng 中等 medium (size)
zhōng guó 中国 China
zhōng guó huà 中国 Chinese painting
zhōng wén 中文 Chinese
zhōng wǔ 中午 noon
zhǒng zhàng 肿胀 swelling
zhòng shǔ 中暑 sunstroke
zhōu mò 周末 weekend
zhǒu 肘 elbow
zhū bǎo shāng 珠宝商 jeweler
zhǔ cài 主菜 main course
zhù sù 住宿 accommodation
zhù shǒu 住手 v stop
zhǔ yào jǐng diǎn 主要景点 main attraction
zhù zài 住在 v stay
zhuān jiā 专家 specialist (doctor)
zhuǎn 转 v transfer (change trains/flights)
zhuǎn jī 转机 connection (flight)
zhuǎn zhàng 转账 v transfer (money)
zhuàng guān 壮观 magnificent
zhuàng 撞 v crash (car)
zhǔn bèi hǎo 准备好 ready
zhuō zi 桌子 table
zhuó zhuāng yāo qiú 着装要求 dress code
zǐ sè 紫色 purple
zì dòng 自动 automatic
zì dòng fú tī 自动扶梯 escala▮
zì dòng qì chē 自动汽车 automatic car
zì dòng qǔ kuǎn jī 自动取款机 ATM
zì rán bǎo hù qū 自然保护区 nature preserve
zì xíng chē 自行车 bicycle
zì xíng chē lù xiàn 自行车路 bike route
zì zhù 自助 self-service
zǒu 走 v walk
zū 租 v rent
zū chē 租车 car rental [hire BE]
zū yòng qì chē 租用汽车 ren▮ [hire BE] car
zú qiú sài 足球赛 soccer [footb▮ BE]
zǔ fù/mǔ 祖父/母 grandparen▮
zuàn shí 钻石 diamond
zuǐ 嘴 mouth
zuǐ chún 嘴唇 lip
zuì hǎo 最好 best
zuì hòu 最后 last
zuó tiān 昨天 yesterday
zuǒ bian 左边 left (direction)
zuò xià 坐下 v sit